THE CHINESE
RESTAURANT
EXPERIENCE

THE CHINESE RESTAURANT EXPERIENCE

Jennie Low
Diane Yee

PRESIDIO PRESS

Published by Presidio Press, 31 Pamaron Way, Novato, CA 94947

Library of Congress Cataloging in Publication Data

Low, Jennie, 1940–
    The Chinese restaurant experience.

    Includes indexes.
    1. San Francisco (Calif.)—Restaurants—Directories.
2. Cookery, Chinese.   I. Yee, Diane, date
II. Title.
TX907.L64   647′.95794′6   81-21055
ISBN 0-89141-155-0   AACR2

Cover design by Kathleen A. Jaeger
Quote on page 6 excerpted with permission from
How to Cook and Eat in Chinese by Buwei Yang Chao,
Random House, Inc., 1963.
Printed in the United States of America

DEDICATION

To all the fine Chinese chefs in the San Francisco Bay Area for their expertise, imagination, and creativity. Because of their contributions, this area is one of the best places in the world for Chinese dining outside of the Orient.

A special thank you to Doong Tien for her conscientious work on the manuscript.

To our families for their assistance, support, and uncomplaining ordeals on "nights out" at many restaurants.

To Eloise C. Auyong and Lauan Garnjost for typing the manuscript.

CONTENTS

INTRODUCTION

In the San Francisco Bay Area, we are indeed fortunate in having the largest concentration of Chinese restaurants outside of the Orient. This is a comprehensive guide to the better of these restaurants. It is our hope that we can assist both locals and newcomers in discovering these restaurants and their particular specialties.

The establishments included are our personal preferences, based on our dining experiences over many years. Readers may have their own favorite places and may question why they have not been included. The answer is simple. We in this area are blessed with many good places to dine, and although we have tried most of them, we cannot write about all of them. Some are in transition periods with new ownership or new head chefs. Others did not exhibit the kind of consistency we prefer. In the future, we will continue to review old restaurants and add new restaurants to our list.

With this book, you can discover the finer Chinese restaurants, and better yet, discover their specialties. There is a constant upgrading of menus as established houses drop unsuccessful dishes and add new ones. There is an infusion of new dishes as chefs are brought in from the Orient. When one restaurant creates a successful new dish, others scramble to copy and improve on it. This book highlights these special dishes, many of which are only on the Chinese menu. For these dishes, the Chinese characters will appear next to the description to assist you in ordering.

Listed with each restaurant are menu suggestions for three meals for four or five persons. The suggested dishes for each meal include the house specialties as well as other dishes to offer a well-balanced, delicious, and nutritious meal. For the diner who wishes to depart from these menus, some guidelines for ordering a Chinese meal are given on pages 7–14.

One of the favorite Chinese culinary traditions is the diem sum or tea lunch, an exquisite array of delicacies. Listed on pages 30–33 are a number of these delicacies and descriptions of them. The experience is a must! It is a feast for the eyes as well as the palate.

Restaurant selections were based primarily on the quality and cost of the food. Ambience and service were secondary considerations.

Chinese food, with its great variety, is best enjoyed when many dishes are available for a meal. Get about ten people together and order eight or nine dishes with a soup for an outstanding dining experience.

We wish you all good eating.

CUISINES

Due to the diverse geography, the different ingredients available to regional cooks, and the variety of climates, many styles of cooking evolved in China. Rather than mention each geographical area, we find it convenient to categorize restaurant cuisines into four major types: Cantonese, Mandarin, Szechuan, and Mongolian.

Dishes originating in southern China are Cantonese. In this area, food is lightly seasoned and steamed or stir-fried. The quick stir-fry method preserves the crispness of vegetables and succulence of meats. Dishes from northern China are generally considered Mandarin and are usually spicier, with stronger flavorings and sauces than in the south. While some "fancier" Mandarin dishes are subtle and mild, others use an abundance of garlic and green onions. Szechuan food has much more zest than most other Chinese cuisines because of the addition of hot peppers, which results in very full-flavored dishes. Lamb and mutton are popularly used in Mongolian cuisine. The people use a Mongolian grill, an indoor barbecue on which small pieces of food are cooked over red-hot charcoal.

Prior to the 1960s, most of the Chinese living in the United States, and therefore most of the chefs, were from southern China, which made Cantonese food the only Chinese cuisine familiar to most Americans. With China's Cultural Revolution in 1963, many chefs fled from all areas of the country, taking with them recipes for the traditional dishes of their provinces. Now American diners can enjoy a large variety of cooking styles, and as chefs borrow, combine, or blend the most dominant features of one cuisine with another, they can expect an even further refinement of the Chinese culinary art.

ABOUT PRICES

Compared to most cuisines, Chinese food is very reasonably priced. This book's "expensive" category is probably equivalent to the "moderate" category for most other cuisines.

To assist you in finding a restaurant to match your budget, we have devised the following simple system. These price categories do not include drinks and tips, and although prices may increase, the relationships among the categories should stay fixed.

$ is **reasonable** (under $5 per person)
$$ is **moderate** (from $6 to $9 per person)
$$$ is **expensive** (more than $10 per person)

Delicious Chinese food can be found in each category, but generally speaking, ambience and service are usually better in the higher price ranges.

SIGNIFICANCE OF FOOD
IN THE CHINESE CULTURE

Man should not eat rice that is affected by the weather, nor fish or meat that is discolored or foul in smell. Vegetables should be fresh and in season; meat should be properly cut, and flavors and tastes should be blended properly.

—"The Analects of Confucius"
(born 551 B.C.)

Chinese cooking and the appreciation of fine foods evolved during the Chou Dynasty (1122 to 1249 B.C.). Confucius, the great and powerful teacher born during that reign, taught the people the humanistic virtues of life, as well as respect for good food. He also established standards on how foods should be eaten. During this time, great importance was placed on religious rituals, public ceremonies, and social festivities. At these occasions, special festival foods were served. The presence of good food was an intrinsic part of being in peace and harmony with oneself and loving others—basic principles of Confucian teaching. The Chinese culinary art is still an intricate part of the Chinese culture. All Chinese people, the old and the young, have a great appreciation and reverence for good food. To them, eating is not just enjoyable. Food is life and health, and is symbolic of other good things, such as luck and prosperity.

The high respect with which the Chinese people regard food is largely due to China's geography. It is one of the largest and most populous countries of the world, yet only 11 percent of the land is cultivable. Most of it is desert or mountains, and the temperatures are extreme, resulting in short growing seasons. The scarcity of cultivable land, combined with harsh weather conditions and lack of fuel, have made starvation a threat for centuries. These diverse conditions have forced the Chinese always to be preoccupied with food. They look everywhere and set no limits on what they find. Such delicacies as lily buds, fungi, sea cucumbers, and bird's nest have become part of the diet. An ancient Chinese gourmet stated, "Every eating material can be made palatable provided that it is given the proper cooking time." The most successful experiments have become part of China's cultural heritage. Buwei Yang Chao in *How to Cook Chinese* comments "that food must have taste or flavor, even though ingredients used may be the most common and inexpensive. It is the art of the cook to create the means to give taste and flavor to food." Imagination combined with an intrinsic sense of artistry is demonstrated in many creations. Each dish must be balanced in complementary flavors and contrasting textures and be esthetically pleasing to the eye.

For centuries, most of China's cultivable land has been used for growing grain to feed the people, a more economical use of land than growing grain for raising beef cattle. Small patches of land are used for growing vegetables, and pigs and poultry are raised for meat because they require little room for grazing. Various salting and drying techniques are used to preserve foods.

Today, Chinese food is world renowned because of its diversity of ingredients, high nutritional value, and low caloric content. Vegetables dominate in most dishes, while lean cuts of meat are used sparingly in them. Grains are plentiful. Chinese prefer crisp, delicate foods to rich, oily ones.

When Chinese gather for a meal, they talk at great length about what they are eating, what they have eaten, and what they are going to eat. Both cooking and eating are activities that are usually participated in by all members of the family. The sharing of good food is a part of the Chinese way of life. A gathering without it is both incomplete and rare.

HOW TO ORDER
A CHINESE LUNCH

Combinations of dishes similar to the dinner suggestions that follow are appropriate for lunch, though fewer are usually ordered. You may also decide on just a bowl of won ton soup or a plate of chow fun or chow mein. A side order of barbecued pork or Chinese greens complements any of these noodle dishes.

For quick service and economy, many restaurants have luncheon plates that include tea. Prices for these are usually much less than for the à la carte dishes because these specials are based on availability of seasonal produce.

HOW TO ORDER
A CHINESE DINNER

The traditional Chinese dinner is best served "family style," rather than a separate entrée for each individual. A "family-style" dinner should include a variety of dishes that offer a well-balanced and nutritious meal. The ideal number for a dinner is four or five persons. For this number, order four to six different dishes with soup and rice and the dishes are shared by all. For eight to ten persons, order two servings of each dish; for two persons, order two dishes with soup and rice.

We have included three suggested menus (with house specialties included) for meals at each restaurant. The selection of dishes is balanced with meats, vegetables, and seafood. Most Cantonese restaurants will include "soup of the day" for no cost to accompany any of the dishes ordered à la carte. Otherwise, choose one of our dinners that includes a soup. Some dinners will have an appetizer before soup.

For single diners, order any dish on the à la carte menu to be served with rice. For example, sweet and sour pork, chicken with snow peas, or beef with greens can be served over hot steamed rice.

The traditional Chinese dinner includes hot steamed rice to blend in with the good flavors of the dishes. Appetizers, wine, and dessert complement any Chinese meal, and hot tea is always served after the meal.

In closing, we'd like to pass on a tip about ordering. Make your selections from the à la carte menu. This will insure that your food will be fresh and cooked to order.

HOW TO ORDER
A CHINESE BANQUET

To truly enjoy the wide variety of Chinese food possible, get about ten people together for a banquet. Select a restaurant where you particularly like the food and order the dishes at least two days in advance. The manager or chef at the restaurant will be glad to assist you in planning a menu.

The cost per person for a banquet is very reasonable, considering eight to ten courses are usually served. Some restaurants have special rooms with elegant place settings and crystal stemware for very special banquets, and many can accommodate large parties.

We are providing a few banquet menus. Most of the suggested dishes can be ordered at any Cantonese or Mandarin restaurant. You may want to substitute a few house specialties for some of our selections.

Try a Chinese banquet at least once. It is a gastronomic feast! Relax and allow at least two hours to enjoy the experience.

Cantonese Banquet Menus for Ten Persons

Menu #1
Bird's Nest Soup
Cantonese Chicken Salad
Peking Duck with Steamed Buns
Steak Cubes with Chinese Greens *or* Snow Peas
Steamed Whole Rock Cod
Crispy Chicken
Crab with Black Bean Sauce (seasonal)
Cashew Nut Prawns
Steamed Rice *or* Fried Rice

Menu #2
Shark's Fin Soup
Chicken with Sweet Rice Stuffing
Peking Duck with Steamed Buns
Clams with Black Bean Sauce
Black, Straw, and Button Mushrooms with Chinese Greens in Oyster Sauce
Sweet and Sour Whole Rock Cod
Steak Cubes with Tender Greens
Mongolian Lamb *or* Beef
Steamed Rice

Menu #3
Whole Winter Melon Soup *or* Diced Winter Melon Soup
Boiled Chicken with Virginia Ham and Chinese Greens
Peking Duck with Steamed Buns
Black Mushrooms and Abalone in Oyster Sauce
Steak Cubes with Tender Greens

Ginger and Green Onion Crab (seasonal) *or* Crystal Prawns
Fresh Scallops with Vegetables
Cantonese Chicken Salad
Steamed Rice

Mandarin Banquet Menus for Ten Persons

Menu #1
Potstickers
Sizzling Rice Soup
Peking Duck with Steamed Buns *or* Smoked Tea Duck
Szechuan Spiced Beef *or* Mongolian Lamb
Kung Pao Chicken
Snow Peas with Prawns
Crab in Black Bean Sauce (seasonal) *or* Clams in Black Bean Sauce
Sweet and Sour Whole Fish
Steamed Rice

Menu #2
Potstickers
Hot and Sour Soup
Mongolian Beef
Mu Shu Pork
Lemon Chicken
Kung Pao Prawns
Abalone in Oyster Sauce
Crab in Black Bean Sauce (seasonal) *or* Clams in Black Bean Sauce
Steamed Rice

MENU #3

Potstickers

Crab Meat Winter Melon Soup

Steak Cubes with Chinese Greens *or* Asparagus Beef (seasonal)

Crispy Duck with Steamed Buns

Hot Bean Cake with Pork

Butterfly Prawns

Steamed Whole Fish with Black Bean Sauce

Spiced Shrimp

Steamed Rice

DESCRIPTIONS
OF POPULAR DISHES

Refer to this list for descriptions of the dishes listed as specialties of the restaurants that follow.

Abalone in Oyster Sauce: 蠔油鮑魚

This is not the fresh abalone one expects. It is cooked, canned abalone from the Orient. Delicious, nevertheless, when cooked with oyster sauce and garnished with slivers of green onion.

Almond Chicken Ding: 杏仁鷄丁

You know almond and you know chicken, but what is "ding"? Ding means diced. This dish combines diced almonds, chicken, celery, peas, onions, etc.

Almond Milk Curd: 杏仁豆腐

Not actually a "curd," but rather a milk-based gelatin dessert. Very similar to jello, with a touch of almond-extract flavoring. Usually served with a few canned lychees or a spoonful of fruit cocktail over it; more expensively served with a jigger of crème de menthe. A cool, refreshing, light dessert.

Almond Pressed Duck: 窩燒香鴨

This duck dish is not "pressed" as in shirts, nor are there many almonds! Duck is first stewed with spices, then the flesh is stripped from the carcass, mixed with tapioca starch and cornstarch, and formed into patties. These are deep-fried to a golden brown and then cut into bite-sized pieces. Served on a bed of lettuce, veiled with sweet and sour sauce, and garnished with crushed almonds, this dish is indeed a delicious mixture of taste and texture, and a visual delight.

Barley Duck (Guo Jee Op): 菓子鴨

Duck is first deep-fried, then stuffed with barley, mushrooms, and meat, and simmered in herbs and spices until tender. Served with a delicious gravy made from the natural juices and topped with coriander.

Bean Cakes, Family Style (Tofu): 紅燒豆腐

Bean cakes cut into cubes, stir-fried with meat, bamboo shoots, mushrooms, or vegetables. This is a bland style of preparing bean cakes, but tasty nevertheless.

Bean Cakes with Ground Pork (Ma Po Tofu): 麻婆豆腐

The bean cake is diced into small pieces, combined with minced meat, peas, and bamboo shoots, and cooked with hot peppers and bean sauce. The contrast of flavors and textures offered by this dish is a gourmet experience.

Beef Stew, Chinese (Gnau Nom): 牛 腩

The Chinese version of beef stew is made from beef brisket, spiced with star anise, and braised with distinctive seasonings until tender. Usually served over soup noodles or rice.

Beef under Snow: 明牛肉

The "snow" is deep-fried rice-stick noodles. They are mounded over slices of beef, which have been stir-fried with vegetables. This is another example of the Chinese culinary art of blending different flavors and different textures.

Bird's Nest Soup: 燕窩湯

If you should see this exotic, delicious soup on any menu, do not hesitate to order it. It is made from the nest of swallows (well cleaned and sterilized) and chicken broth. One of the marvels of Chinese cuisine, it demonstrates the imagination and great lengths that man will go to for sustenance.

Bok Choy (Tender Greens, Chinese Greens): 白　菜

A unique Chinese vegetable, somewhere between broccoli and Swiss chard in flavor and texture. Usually stir-fried with beef, chicken, or prawns, or sometimes by itself.

Butterfly Prawns: 鐵扒明蝦

Whole prawns, filleted and flavored with pieces of bacon, dipped in a light batter and deep-fried. The prawns are served on a bed of lettuce, and are eaten with mustard, ketchup, and a touch of lemon. This is one of the most demanding dishes to prepare because swiftness between the moment of cooking and serving is essential.

Chicken Salad, Cantonese: 手撕鷄

Oh, what a delight! Unlike the western chicken salad with which we are familiar, the Cantonese version is a masterful blend of taste, texture, and visual appeal. Slivers of hand-shredded, roasted chicken are combined with lettuce, celery, and green onions. Deep-fried rice sticks, peanuts, and sesame seeds are added. A touch of coriander adds its delightful taste, along with a unique blend of seasonings—sesame oil, flavored salt, sugar, soy sauce, a touch of plum sauce, and absolutely no mayonnaise. A great dish as a salad course or as an entrée by itself.

Chicken with Sweet Rice Stuffing: 糯米鷄

This dish represents a real test of the culinary skills of the Chinese chef. First, the entire skeleton of the chicken is removed, leaving the flesh and skin intact as much as possible. Next the fowl is stuffed with sweet rice that has been cooked with bits of mushroom, dried shrimp, green onion, and Chinese sausage. Batter is applied and the entire stuffed bird is deep-fried to a golden brown. The flattened, stuffed bird is cut into bite-sized pieces and served on a bed of shredded lettuce with a sliced lemon half.

Chicken with Virginia Ham: 鴛鴦鷄

A banquet favorite. A whole chicken is simmered to perfection in a pot of broth, then cut into bite-sized pieces and placed on a bed of greens, usually Chinese broccoli. Between each piece of fowl, a thin slice of very expensive Virginia ham is placed. Hot chicken gravy is poured over the entire dish. Great with steamed rice.

Chinese Mustard: 芥　末

Caution: Chinese mustard is *hot.* It is meant to be used sparingly on meats, fowl, or shellfish.

Chow Fun (Chinese Rice Noodles): 炒　粉

This is a variation of chow mein, made with flat, wide rice noodles instead of egg noodles. A blander, more filling dish than chow mein, it is usually available in the same variations of beef, pork, chicken, or shrimp and is more favored by the Chinese. Difficult to find outside of Chinatown.

Clams in Black Bean Sauce: 鼓汁大蜆

Fresh clams, stir-fried in the shell. The sweet taste of clam is combined with black bean and garlic sauce—A far cry from steamed clams served with butter!

Clams in Ginger and Garlic Sauce: 生炒大蜆

Another method of preparing clams. Ginger and garlic are often used in the Chinese cooking of seafoods for a good reason. Any "fishy" taste is dispelled by them. Also, these two spices, used judiciously, blend beautifully with the sweetness of fresh shellfish.

Clay Pot: 煲仔菜

In some Chinese restaurants you will find clay-pot dishes on the menu. Clay-pot cooking is just that: meat, fowl, or vegetable combinations cooked in a traditional pot of clay. This method of cooking seals in all the natural juices, and since the pot is a heat-retaining vessel, the food comes to the table sizzling hot. Braised chicken, tofu with mixed vegetables, mushrooms with abalone, and beef brisket are typically cooked in clay pots. Great in cold weather.

Congee (Jook): 粥

Congee is the Chinese version of porridge, or gruel. It is basically a rice soup, cooked to thick or thin consistency, as desired. Chicken, pork, or fish are added for flavor. After Thanksgiving, turkey congee is a standard in many Chinese homes. Congee is eaten as a light lunch or a late-evening snack. It is a perfect repast after an evening out because it is light, but still filling. Chopped green onions, ginger, minced ham or pork, and chopped lettuce are common accompaniments. A deep-fried Chinese doughnut, called yau jow gwai (literally "oil-fried ghost," for some inexplicable reason), is often eaten with congee.

Crab in Black Bean Sauce: 豉汁大蟹

This is a seasonal dish, messy to eat because the crab is cooked in the shell. Whole fresh crab is chopped into pieces and stir-fried with black bean sauce. For those who like crab, this is a "must-try." If black bean is not your flavor, then order crab with ginger and green onion, or for the real gourmet, curried crab.

Crab with Meat and Egg Sauce: 芙蓉大蟹

Cooked much the same as above, but with chopped meat and eggs combined into a smooth sauce. Delicious over rice.

Crispy Chicken: 脆皮鷄

Although similar to fried chicken, fried chicken this is not! Rather, it is elaborately prepared chicken, moist and tasty, with a crusty skin. Prepared this way, chicken is practically fat free, unlike chicken that has been fried.

Crystal Prawns: 玻璃蝦球

Large prawns prepared a special way, so that upon serving, they have the appearance of quality crystal, hence the name. Prawns are treated, deep-fried briefly, then stir-fried with vegetables, cashew nuts, or both.

Curried Chicken: 咖喱鷄

Try this dish, if only to introduce yourself to the Chinese way of "curry cooking." It differs from the usual method in that no milk is used, and pieces of celery and onions add to the flavor of the curry. Usually prepared heavy on the curry, so you should caution the cook if you prefer it milder.

Dried Scallop Soup: 江瑤柱湯

A thick, tasty soup that derives its flavor from dried scallops. The scallops are shredded and then combined with slivered bamboo shoots, mushrooms, and chicken. An egg, beaten and added at the last moment, lends a smooth texture to the soup.

Duck's Feet: 鴨　脚

Eat the feet of the duck? Preposterous? Not at all! Did you know that duck and chicken feet come with a natural pair of socks? This "sock," or leathery covering, is "peeled" off before final preparation of the feet. Thus, the Chinese have discovered a real taste treat waddling around in the barnyard! You can discover it, too. The duck feet are stewed with Chinese seasonings.

Egg Foo Young: 芙蓉蛋

"Foo young" is short for "foo young don," which means "egg omelet." The foo young is made with bean sprouts and yellow onions. Crab foo young is simply a Chinese egg omelet with fresh or canned crab meat. Foo young may be served with or without a gravy.

Fish, Braised with Brown Bean Sauce: 紅燒魚

Fish is pan-fried, then simmered in a spicy brown bean sauce. Delicious with rice.

Fish, Steamed (Whole): 清蒸魚

Steamed fish is definitely a favorite among the Chinese, both in taste and in concept. The fish is steamed and served whole, and it is the perfect complement to a bowl of hot rice.

Fish, Steamed with Black Bean Sauce: 豉汁蒸魚

Basically, this is prepared in the same manner as the above fish, with the addition of black bean sauce. Recommended for preparation for bland-tasting fish, such as rock cod.

Fish, Steamed with Ginger and Green Onion: 羗葱蒸魚

The most common style of preparation for steamed fish, it is garnished with slivered ginger and green onions. Just prior to serving, hot vegetable oil and soy sauce are poured over it. This makes it very smooth in flavor, but more importantly, rids it of any "fishy" taste.

Fish with Sweet and Sour Sauce: 甜酸魚

The whole fish is slashed, dipped in batter, and deep-fried. Then a delicious sweet and sour sauce, with chopped onions, peas, carrots, and sweet pickles, is poured over the fish before serving. Definitely enjoyed by fans of "sweet and sour sauce."

Fried Squid: 炸油魚

The Chinese version of "calamari." The squid is marinated with Chinese seasonings, dipped in a light batter, and deep-fried.

Hot and Sour Soup: 酸辣湯

This should more accurately be called "sour and hot soup," for that is the way it translates from the Chinese. By some quirk, it is almost universally called "hot and sour soup." The "hot" refers to its spiciness, not temperature. Combined with a slightly vinegary taste, this soup does wonders for perking up one's appetite. It is one of the few thick soups in the Chinese repertoire and many ingredients, such as wood ears, bamboo shoots, bean curd, golden needles, and chicken, are used in the broth.

King Du Spareribs: 京都排骨

See *Mandarin Spareribs.*

Kung Pao Chicken: 宮保鷄

Diced chicken is stir-fried with bamboo shoots, snow peas, hot peppers, green peppers, and deep-fried peanuts, then covered with a sauce.

Kung Pao Prawns: 宮保蝦

Same as above, substituting prawns for chicken.

Lobster in Black Bean Sauce: 豉汁龍蝦

A word about lobster. Fresh lobster is a food prized by the Chinese, but, as you know, it is very expensive. Should your pocket book allow, however, do try lobster cooked in the Chinese way! Compared with the western method of boiling and dipping in butter, the Chinese method is far superior. Be forewarned: Chinese-style lobster may be a bit messy to eat, but the experience is worth the effort. In this method, it is prepared with pungent black bean sauce.

Lotus Root with Pork: 蓮藕小炒

A Cantonese dish of lotus root stir-fried with celery, snow peas, preserved radish, and pork slices. The lotus root lends an unusual crunchy texture to this dish.

Mandarin Glazed Apples or Bananas: 拔絲香蕉，蘋果

A dessert from northern China. Fresh pieces of apple or banana are coated with a very light batter and then fried. Then they are dipped in hot syrup and crystallized by dipping into ice water at the table.

Mandarin Spareribs: 北京排骨

These are similar to "sweet and sour spareribs," but not the same. Meaty ribs are first deep-fried, then lightly covered with sweet and sour sauce.

Minced Squab: 炒白鴿鬆

This is the Chinese "taco." Squab (or ground pork) is finely minced, along with water chestnuts, mushrooms, celery, and bamboo shoots, then stir-fried. Served with a large platter of lettuce leaves and hoisin sauce. The mixture is spooned onto a lettuce leaf, flavored with hoisin sauce, rolled up taco style, and eaten.

Mongolian Beef: 蒙古牛肉

Beef slices stir-fried in a spicy sauce with shredded vegetables or green onions.

Mongolian Fire Pot (Huo Kuo, Da Bin Low): 打邊爐

This is the Oriental version of fondue, using chicken stock in place of cheese sauce or hot oil. Platters of fish, fowl, beef, and vegetables are provided. Each diner selects what he or she wants from the platters, places the selections in a small wire basket, and cooks them in the common "fire pot" of chicken stock. The traditional charcoal-fueled fire pot, or even the modern electric version, provides plenty of warmth at the table, so this dish is a favorite for cold winter nights. The best part comes at the end, when the broth, by now doubly flavored by the meat, fish, fowl, and vegetables cooked in it, is consumed.

Mongolian Lamb: 蒙古羊肉

Same as above, but substituting lamb.

Mu Shu Pork: 木樨肉

This northern Chinese dish is the Oriental version of the Mexican burrito. A filling of chopped pork, vegetables, and eggs is stir-fried and served with thin flour pancakes. The mixture, along with hoisin sauce and slivered green onions, is spooned onto the pancake, folded burrito style, and eaten.

Mun Yee Mein: 鴻圖伊麵

Egg noodles are first deep-fried, then served in a thick gravy containing a variety of meats and vegetables.

Mun Yee Mein, Sub Gum: 什碎伊麵

This is the house special, and usually contains pieces of chicken, barbecued pork, squid, Chinese greens, prawns, etc.

Mushrooms in Oyster Sauce: 蠔油冬菇

The dried black Chinese mushroom, quite different from the familiar button mushroom, is a favorite in cooking. Because it is very expensive, it is used sparingly, usually in minced or sliced form. Occasionally, a mushroom dish is served, usually at banquets, containing three types of mushrooms (black, straw, and button) that have been gently simmered in oyster sauce, then garnished with green onions.

Pan-fried Prawns in Shell: 椒鹽大蝦

The Chinese cook shellfish in the shell for a very good reason. It retains the sweetness and the juices. The shellfish, combined with flavorings, make delicious eating. It takes a little effort to remove the shell, but the taste experience makes the work worthwhile.

Paper-wrapped Chicken
(Parchment Chicken, Foil-wrapped Chicken): 紙包鷄

Why wrap a piece of chicken in foil for cooking? It results in a juicy, tasty morsel when deep-fried. All of the natural juices and marinade are retained in the packet during the cooking process. Another method is to use an edible pastry dough, thin and parchmentlike, as a wrapper. No messy unwrapping. Just eat the whole thing! Beef is also prepared this way.

Pei Pa Duck: 琵琶鴨

This is the duck one sees hanging in many Chinatown shop windows. The names translates as "duck in the shape of the pei-pa," or Chinese lute. This preparation falls somewhere between roast duck and Peking duck. It has the taste and moistness of the former, but the skin more nearly approaches the crispy texture of the latter.

Peking Duck: 北京鴨

Most people have heard of Peking duck, but very few know how it is prepared or eaten. The preparation requires two days. The whole duckling is first dipped in honey and water, then hung to dry overnight. This procedure rids the duck of its fat and prepares the skin. The duck is then barbecued, basting often, until the skin is golden brown and crackling in texture. Ideally, the pieces of crackling skin are carved first and served. Then the flesh is carved and the pieces are placed between layers of a steamed bun, garnished with slivers of green onion and plum sauce, and eaten. Unfortunately, this method of serving requires much time and labor, so restaurants do not often serve it in this manner. Rather, the duck is merely cut into serving pieces, and the diner is left the chore of stripping the skin and flesh from the bone in order to prepare his own sandwich.

Peking Spareribs: 京都排骨

See *Mandarin Spareribs.*

Pork Hash (Hom Ngee Yuk): 鹹魚猪肉餅

An old favorite in Chinese homes, this is a pungent but very flavorful and satisfying preparation of pork steamed with salted fish. The combination, when eaten with steamed rice, is indescribably delicious.

Potstickers (Kuo Teh): 鍋　貼

Small dumplings filled with a delicate meat and vegetable stuffing, grilled crisp on one side, served with vinegar, soy sauce, and hot pepper oil.

Raw Fish Salad: 魚　生

Over fifteen ingredients are combined with slivers of boneless fish (usually soong yeu, preferred because of its mild flavor). Like Chinese chicken salad, this is not a salad in the western sense, and it is rarely found in restaurants. Often times, it must be ordered a day or two in advance, and it is usually available only during the winter season. In San Francisco, both Sun Hung Heung and Asia Garden prepare this delicacy. At Sam Wo's (also in San Francisco), it is a standard menu item. Congee, a natural accompaniment to raw fish salad, is available here, too.

Scallops, Stir-fried: 生炒帶子

When the scallops are fresh, and the chef is quick, there is no greater dish. The sweetness of fresh scallops, quickly stir-fried with sweet peas, produces a dish fit for royalty.

Shark's Fin Soup: 魚翅湯

An even rarer delicacy than bird's nest soup. Gelatinous threads of the shark's fin, combined with shreds of chicken meat, are used to make this soup. Because of the scarcity of sharks, and the amount of labor involved in this preparation, it is very expensive, about $5 per serving. For the gourmet palate, it's worth the price.

Shrimp with Lobster Sauce: 龍蝦球糊

This dish requires some explaining. There is shrimp, but no lobster. "Lobster sauce" refers to the sauce, a mixture of black beans, meat, and eggs, originally used in cooking lobsters. The very high price of lobster has resulted, understandably, in the substitution of shrimp with this sauce.

Sizzling Rice Prawns: 鍋巴蝦

Prawns, green pepper, onion, bamboo shoots, and bean sprouts are served in a sweet and sour sauce over deep-fried rice patties. Listen to the sizzle as the prawn mixture is poured over the rice patties.

Sizzling Rice Soup: 鍋巴湯

This is one of the "show" dishes in the Chinese repertoire. The hot soup, containing chicken, abalone, shrimp, snow peas, water chestnuts, and bamboo shoots, is brought to the table along with a platter of crisp rice patties. Then the two are combined, producing a tempting "sizzle" that sells the soup.

Smoked Tea Duck: 樟茶鴨

A whole young duck is marinated in tea leaves for several days, then barbecued in a smoke oven. The duck is deep-fried to a golden brown just before serving. The duck pieces are usually served with steamed buns.

Soy Sauce Chicken: 豉油鷄

Whole chicken cooked in a flavored soy sauce. These chickens can be seen hanging along with roast duck in Chinatown shop windows. When properly cooked, the flesh is moist and succulent, with a slightly sweet soy-sauce flavor. Definitely a dish to be accompanied with rice.

Spiced Crispy Duck: 香酥鴨

Another version of Peking duck, but deep-fried instead of roasted. Also served with hot steamed buns and green onions.

Spiced Prawns: 宮保明蝦

Differ from deep-fried prawns in that a spicy hot sauce is added to the prawns after deep-frying. The sauce is made from hot peppers and other condiments. Deep-fried prawns are best eaten with hot mustard and ketchup; spiced prawns are ready to eat just as they are.

Steak Cubes: 炒市的球

Pieces of tenderized beef steak are cut into bite-sized pieces and briefly fried in the wok, then quickly stir-fried with fresh vegetables. Some restaurants prepare this dish with tomatoes and hoisin sauce, resulting in a sweeter version.

Steamed Dumplings (Hsiao Loong Bau): 小籠包

Small dumplings from the North, made with a soft flour dough and stuffed with a meat filling. All of the rich meat juices are enclosed in the dumpling. Use chili oil and soy sauce as condiments.

Suey Gow Soup: 水餃湯

A dumpling in soup, differing from won tons. Suey gow are first steamed, then served in broth. They are larger than won tons, so not as many are required per serving. Found in only a few restaurants.

Szechuan Spiced Beef: 四川牛肉

Shredded beef, bamboo shoots, hot peppers, green peppers, and sliced turnips stir-fried in a spicy sauce. Delightful in cold weather.

Twice-cooked Pork: 回鍋肉

Slices of tenderloin pork boiled, then stir-fried in a spicy sauce with Chinese vegetables.

Velvet Chicken: 生炒鷄片

Tender fillets of chicken breast stir-fried with snow peas, water chestnuts, and bamboo shoots, served in a delicious sauce.

West Lake Duck (Stewed Duck): 西湖鴨

Literally "duck of the West Lake." A very popular dish, the duck is first deep-fried, then simmered in herbs and spices until tender. Served with a delicious gravy made from the natural juices and topped with coriander.

Winter Melon Soup: 冬瓜粒湯

The classic winter melon soup is prepared with the whole melon. The seeds are scooped out and the cavity is filled with bits of chicken, bamboo shoots, mushrooms, lotus seeds, and sometimes even bird's nest! Then the whole melon is set into the wok and steamed for three to four hours. The result is a delicious soup flavored by the melon's flesh. It is served at table by gently carving pieces of the melon into each serving. The economy version of this soup is made with diced pieces of winter melon instead of the whole melon.

Won Tons: 雲　吞

Deep-fried won tons: Served with a sweet and sour sauce as an appetizer or as one course of a lunch or dinner.

Hung tao yee won tons: Deep-fried won tons are put in a thick soup that contains peas, bamboo shoots, and mushrooms together with minced barbecued pork.

Wor won tons: Boiled won tons served in a soup brimming with pieces of fresh prawns, squid, chicken meat and livers, snow peas, bamboo shoots, and mushrooms.

Yee won tons: These won tons are first deep-fried, then served in a broth. There are different varieties, such as barbecued pork, chicken, shrimp, etc.

DIEM SUM
(CHINESE TEA LUNCH)

The little delights served at a tea lunch are called diem sum, which translates "touch your heart," and this is indeed what these morsels do. The tea lunch is a favorite culinary tradition with the Chinese. It is pleasant to nibble on a series of small delicacies, while leisurely sipping tea and enjoying friends. People in the San Francisco Bay Area are fortunate to have several excellent diem sum restaurants, many patterned after the great tea parlors of the Orient, to choose from.

It is fun to observe the hustle and bustle in these restaurants, usually huge, mess-hall-type dining rooms, filled with chattering people, pretty Chinese girls announcing their trays of delicacies, and long wating lines in the entryway. Don't let the lines discourage you; the experience and food is worth the wait. The restaurants are efficiently organized to move the lines through quickly, and some have a second floor just as large as the first. Tea lunches are usually served from 10:00 A.M. to 3:00 P.M. A greater selection of delicacies and prompter seating can be expected before the crowds start at noon on weekdays and before 11:00 A.M. on weekends. If you are in a hurry, however, you can purchase diem sum to take home.

Upon being seated, the waitress will ask what kind of tea you want. Most local Chinese order po nay, but you can refer to the list of teas and their descriptions on page 35 for other choices. Incidentally, when your teapot is empty and you are ready for a refill, signal the waitress by merely turning the cover upside down or on its side.

There is no need to ask for a menu. The food will come to you automatically. It is served on small plates and in bamboo steamers that are carried on trays or rolled out on carts to the diners. Choose anything your heart fancies by merely signaling, nodding your head, or pointing. Verbal communication need only be minimal. Choose sparingly from each selection because there will be many trays coming from the kitchen. Sip your tea, relax, and talk with the other members of your party while you wait for more trays to pass before you. At the end of the meal, the waitress will count the number of serving dishes and steamers on your table and charge accordingly.

Some restaurants place small saucers next to your plate. These are for condiments, such as soy sauce or hot pepper oil. You may also request hot mustard. If you prefer your food spicy, mix a few drops of the hot pepper oil in the soy sauce, then dip the savory delicacies into the mixture.

A list of some of the most common kinds of diem sum and their descriptions follows. Remember that there are usually at least twenty to forty varieties available at any restaurant. You may also want to order won ton soup, chow mein, chow fun, or rice casseroles as part of your diem sum lunch.

Diem Sum Specialties

Barbecued Pork Buns, Baked
(Gop Cha Siu Bau)
焗 叉 燒 飽

Baked buns with barbecued pork and yellow onion filling.

Barbecued Pork Buns, Steamed
(Jing Cha Siu Bau)
蒸 叉 燒 飽

Steamed buns with barbecued pork filling.

Beef Meatballs
(Ngow Yuk Kau)
西菜牛肉賣

Ground beef, orange peel, and seasonings; steamed.

Black Bean Spareribs
(See Jup Pai Gwut)
鼓 汁 排 骨

Pieces of seasoned spareribs, steamed with black bean sauce and green onions.

Chinese Doughnuts
(Jeen Dui)
煎　　堆

Glutinous rice flour dumplings filled with sweet bean paste, coated with sesame seeds, and deep-fried.

Custard Cups
(Don Tot)
蛋　　撻

Chinese custard tarts.

Duck's Feet
(Op Gurk)
鹵 水 鴨 脚

Duck's feet stewed with Chinese spices.

Egg Rolls
(Choon Guen)
春　　捲

Pork, barbecued pork, bamboo shoots, bean sprouts, and green onion wrapped in pastry skins; deep-fried.

Half-Moon Dumplings
(Fun Gor)
粉　　菓

Wheat starch dumplings filled with carrots, peas, ground pork, and shrimp; steamed.

Paper-wrapped Chicken
(Gee-Bow Gai)
紙 包 鷄

Pieces of marinated chicken wrapped in foil and deep-fried.

Pickled Mustard Greens
(Shuen Guy Choy)
甜 酸 芥 菜

Sweet and sour in taste; crunchy in texture.

Pork Dumplings
(Gee Yuk Shiu Mai)
猪 肉 燒 賣

Dumplings filled with chopped mushrooms and ground pork; steamed.

Pork Triangles
(Hon Sui Gok)
鹹 水 角

Rice flour dumplings filled with ground pork, barbecued pork, bamboo shoots, and shrimp; deep-fried.

Rice Casserole with Chicken
(Gai Fon)
鷄 飯

Rice with chicken, mushrooms, and Chinese sausage; cooked and served in a casserole.

Rice Casserole with Spareribs
(Pai Gwut Fon)
排 骨 飯

Rice with spareribs and black beans; cooked and served in a casserole.

Rice Rolls
(Gnaw Mai Guen)
糯 米 捲

Sweet rice wrapped in pastry skins and deep-fried.

Shrimp Dumplings
(Har Gow)
蝦 餃

Wheat starch dumplings filled with shrimp and bamboo shoots; steamed.

Stuffed Bean Cakes
(Yeung Dow Foo)
釀 豆 腐

Bean cakes stuffed with shrimp paste; pan-fried and served in a light gravy.

Stuffed Bell Pepper
(Yeung Laht Jiu)
釀 青 椒

Bell pepper stuffed with minced shrimp; pan-fried and served in a gravy.

Stuffed Rice Flour Rolls
(Guen Fun)

卷　　粉

Rice flour rolls stuffed with barbecued pork, shrimp, or beef; steamed and served with dark soy sauce.

Sweet Rice with Chicken Wrapped in Lotus Leaf
(Gnaw Mai Gai)

糯　米　鶏

Glutinous rice, pork, chestnuts, peanuts, shrimp, and mushrooms wrapped in lotus leaves; steamed.

Taro Triangles
(Oo Gok)

芋　　角

Taro triangles filled with ground pork, bamboo shoots, green onion, and shrimp; deep-fried.

Chinese Teas to Accompany a Diem Sum Lunch

"Tea tempers the spirits, calms and harmonizes the mind; it arouses thought and prevents drowsiness, lightens and refreshes the body, and clears the perceptive faculties."

—Lu Yu
(800 A.D.)

Chinese tea is an appropriate beverage to accompany a Chinese meal. When drunk before a meal, it clears the palate. When it accompanies a meal, the delicate flavor and taste blend harmoniously with the food. It is served throughout a meal to refresh the diner and to make him or her more receptive to each new course. Tea served after the meal cleanses the palate.

According to legend, tea was discovered accidentally when Emperor Chien Lung was sipping boiled water in his garden, a leaf fell into his cup, and he liked the pleasant, stimulating taste. The Chinese people first cultivated tea for use as an everyday drink in 350 A.D. Turks brought Chinese tea to the Arabs in the seventh century. It wasn't until the sixteenth century that it was first transported to Holland and England. As a result of this introduction, it became a favorite beverage throughout Europe and the world.

Chinese teas are much milder and more delicate in flavor than Indian teas. A single teaspoon is poured into six cups of boiling water. To really appreciate its pure, clean, fresh taste, drink it without cream and sugar.

Though they vary greatly in flavor, smell, and character, Chinese teas all come from the same fragrant plant, *Thea sinensis*, which belongs to the camellia family. There are over 250 varieties of tea and the physical conditions and processing systems make each unique.

There are three major classifications of Chinese tea:

Green tea is unfermented and receives little handling. The young, tenderest leaves from the top of the tree are picked and dried immediately. It is grayish green in color and makes a pale, golden brew. Green tea is refreshing and delicate in taste, good with bland foods.

Black tea is fermented when its leaves have withered from the bush. It is picked, rolled, fermented, and dried. Fermentation changes the color from green to brownish black and strengthens its flavor. Black tea develops a rich, red color and has a strong, pungent aroma. Very good in winter and an excellent accompaniment with deep-fried foods.

Oolong tea is a semifermented tea (partly dried and partly fermented). Fermentation is stopped when the leaves are brownish green. This tea produces an amber brew that is a happy medium between the aroma of black tea and the delicate properties of green tea. Good all-purpose tea because it complements most foods; the most commonly served dinner tea.

Teas Usually Found in Diem Sum Restaurants

This list is organized according to degree of mildness, the mildest teas being listed first.

Dragon Well: From Hangchow. Green tea, unfermented. Has a light, fresh flavor. Famous for its smooth, soothing quality. Considered the finest tea; often served at banquets.

Sui Sen (Water Nymph): From Kwangtung. Green tea; unfermented, refreshing, light, and pleasant. Named for its exquisite aroma. Good mid-morning drink.

Oolong (Black Dragon): From Taiwan, Foochow, and Canton. Semi-fermented; medium bodied. Cross between green and black tea. Delicate flavor and piquant taste. Good for everyday, all-purpose drinking. Best grades are straw-colored brew; lower grades are brown or red.

Look On: Slightly more fermented than oolong. Cross between oolong and po nay. Also good with diem sum.

Po Nay: From Yunnan. Fermented; pungent, full-bodied, dark red brew. Good with deep-fried foods and diem sum.

These are popular scented teas that can be ordered in tea houses and some restaurants.

Jasmine: From Taiwan. Lightly fermented; scented with jasmine blossoms (often oolong with jasmine buds). Light yellow, delicate, and fragrant. Good afternoon tea or between meals.

Lychee: From Taiwan. Oolong or black tea with lychee blossoms. Semi-fermented; sweetly scented tea with aroma of the lychee fruit and a faintly sweet taste.

Chrysanthemum: From Chekiang. Dragon well tea with chrysanthemum petals. Fragrant; taken with Chinese pastry. Chrysanthemum petals are very expensive; considered flowers of immortality, formerly dried for Chinese rulers. Best grades have large flowers. Slightly bittersweet.

Diem Sum
Restaurants

There are no credit cards or reservations taken at any of the following restaurants. For those establishments listed that do not exclusively serve tea lunches, these policies may not apply except during the hours specified.

SAN FRANCISCO

Asia Garden
772 Pacific Avenue (near Stockton)
Telephone: (415) 398-5112
Hours:
    9:00 A.M.–3:00 P.M., daily
Large and popular.

Canton Tea House
1108 Stockton Street (near Jackson)
Telephone: (415) 982-1030
Hours:
    7:30 A.M.–4:00 P.M.. daily
Large and popular.

Grand Palace
950 Grant Avenue (near Jackson)
Telephone: (415) 982-3705
Hours:
    9:30 A.M.–3:00 P.M., daily

Hong Kong Tea House
835 Pacific Street (near Stockton)
Telephone: (415) 391-6365
Hours:
    9:00 A.M.–3:00 P.M., daily

Ruby Palace
631 Kearny Street (near Washington)
Telephone: (415) 433-3196
Hours:
      11:30 A.M.–2:30 P.M., Monday–Friday
      11:00 A.M.–2:30 P.M., Saturday and Sunday
Diem sum is served upstairs only.

Tung Fong
808 Pacific Street (near Stockton)
Telephone: (415) 362-7115
Hours:
      9:00 A.M.–3:00 P.M., Thursday–Tuesday
Small but popular.

Yank Sing
671 Broadway Street (near Stockton)
Telephone: (415) 781-1111
Hours:
      10:00 A.M.–5:00 P.M., daily
Oldest and popular.

53 Stevenson Street (between 1st and 2nd)
Telephone: (415) 495-4510
Hours:
      11:00 A.M.–3:00 P.M., Monday–Friday
Light, cheerful room; skylight and brick walls.

OAKLAND

Tin's Tea House
701 Webster Street
Telephone: (415) 832-5049
Hours:
      9:00 A.M.—3:00 P.M., Monday–Friday
      9:00 A.M.–4:00 P.M., Saturday and Sunday
Modern and cozy.

RESTAURANTS

San Francisco

ASIA GARDEN $$

772 Pacific Avenue (near Stockton)
San Francisco
Telephone: (415) 398-5112
Cuisine: Cantonese

Hours:
    9:00 A.M.–3:00 P.M., diem sum daily
    5:00 P.M.–10.00 P.M., dinner daily

Credit cards: AE, DC, Visa; dinner hours only
Full bar
Reservations recommended for dinner on weekends

Asia Garden is one of those bustling diem sum houses that brims to capacity during the lunch hours. The atmosphere in the evening is more tranquil and relaxing, with soft music, dim lighting, linen napery, and a candle on each table.

Do try the raw fish salad here. Over twenty ingredients are blended with bite-sized pieces of lettuce to create this dish. If you prefer poultry, try the chicken salad, which contains many of the same ingredients.

This restaurant is popular with the local Chinese for banquets and large parties, so be sure to reserve on weekends.

Specialties

Sweet and Sour Pork Chops: Deep-fried pork chops with sweet and sour
   sauce. One of the best versions in town.
Peking Duck (one day advance notice)
Crispy Chicken
Simmered Chicken in Clay Pot: Pieces of chicken simmered in a very deli-
   cate sauce.
Fish Salad (one day advance notice)
Cantonese Chicken Salad

MENU #1
Bird's Nest Soup

Cantonese Chicken Salad

Prawns in Black Bean Sauce

Beef Cubes with Tender Greens

Simmered Chicken in Clay Pot

Steamed Rice

MENU #2
Sweet Corn Soup with Minced Chicken

Sweet and Sour Pork Chops

Crystal Prawns *or* Crab in Black Bean Sauce (seasonal)

Snow Peas with Chicken

Mongolian Beef

Steamed Rice

MENU #3
Diced Winter Melon Soup

Scallops with Mixed Vegetables

Clams in Black Bean Sauce

Beef with Chinese Greens

Crispy Chicken (order a half chicken)

Steamed Rice

BOW HON $$

850 Grant Avenue (near Washington)
San Francisco
Telephone: (415) 362-0601
Cuisine: Cantonese

Hours:
    9:00 A.M.–9:00 P.M., Friday–Wednesday

No credit cards

The clay pots for sale in the window signal the specialty of the house. Clay-pot cooking, popular in China during the cold, wintry months, retains the heat and flavor of foods and is very nutritious because no oil is used. Bow Hon can be credited with introducing clay-pot-style dishes to San Francisco.

There is also a number of other things served here, such as congee, noodles, won tons, and rice-plate lunches. The eating area looks small, but walk toward the kitchen, up the flight of stairs and behold: a larger dining room awaits you on the second floor. This room is a favorite with the Chinese dinner crowd.

Specialities

Mandarin Spareribs 京都排骨
Pan-fried Prawns
Clay-Pot Dishes
King Du Beef with Chinese Greens: Filleted beef stir-fried in hoisin sauce
    with bok choy.

Lunch Menu Recommendations

Won Ton Soup
Shredded Chicken Chow Mein or Chow Fun
Sum See Chow Mein: Bean sprouts, barbecued pork, chicken, and bamboo
    shoots stir-fried with pan-fried noodles.
Fried Vermicelli, Singapore Style: Rice-stick noodles stir-fried with
    chicken, bean sprouts, mushrooms, and bamboo shoots and seasoned
    with curry.

Menu #1
Peking Spareribs
Pan-fried Prawns
Chicken with Chinese Long Beans (seasonal) *or* Chicken with Chinese Greens
Bean Cake with Assorted Meats (in clay pot)
Beef in Oyster Sauce
Steamed Rice

Menu #2
Mongolian Beef
Shrimp with Black Bean Sauce
Stuffed Bean Cake with Peas and Mushrooms (in clay pot)
Sizzling Chicken in Gravy (in clay pot)
Steamed Rock Cod
Steamed Rice

Menu #3
Sweet and Sour Whole Rock Cod
Chicken with Chinese Mushrooms
King Du Beef with Chinese Greens
Sum See with Oyster Sauce (thin slices of barbecued pork, chicken, mushrooms, and bamboo shoots)
Steamed Rice

CANTON TEA HOUSE $$

1108 Stockton Street (near Jackson)
San Francisco
Telephone: (415) 982-1032
Cuisine: Cantonese

Hours:
7:30 A.M.–9:30 P.M., daily

No credit cards

Though open only a few years, this restaurant has definitely caught on. Just about anyone in Chinatown can tell you where the Canton Tea House is located. It is best known for its outstanding tea lunches, but the dinners here are also superb.

The Hong-Kong-trained chef conjures up fantastic dishes in the style of his former home. Try the pei pa up, similar to Peking duck but more delicate in flavor. The Canton special chicken can be found in no other local restaurant. The first layer on the plate is chicken wings that have been marinated in a special sauce, coated with water chestnut flour, and deep-fried to a golden brown. The wings are topped with tender pieces of chicken stir-fried with Chinese greens and mushrooms, then mixed with a thick, brown gravy. One of our dinner guests found the chef's touch with clams in black bean sauce so magnificent, he kept ordering more.

The good-sized, always bustling dining rooms on two floors are reminiscent of the large restaurants in the Orient. Service is quick and efficient. This is definitely one of our favorites.

Specialties

Canton Special Chicken: Pieces of boned chicken stir-fried with mushrooms and Chinese greens and served amidst a circle of deep-fried chicken wings.
Roast Duck
Cooked Lettuce with Oyster Sauce
Braised Whole Rock Cod with Sweet and Sour Sauce
Pei Pa Duck (one day advance notice) 琵琶鴨
Clams in Black Bean Sauce

Menu #1

Sub Gum Winter Melon Soup (diced chicken, bamboo shoots, peas, water chestnuts, and winter melon)

Sautéed Scallops and Prawns

Roast Duck *or* Kung Pao Chicken

Cooked Lettuce with Oyster Sauce *or* Asparagus with Oyster Sauce (seasonal)

Steamed Rice

MENU #2

Mandarin Spareribs

Sirloin Steak Cubes with Tender Greens

Crab Meat with Chinese Broccoli

Canton Special Chicken

Steamed Rice

MENU #3

Beef and Vegetable Soup

Egg Rolls

Mongolian Beef

Scallops with Black Bean Sauce

Shrimp and Abalone with Mushrooms

Steamed Rice

CHINA WEST $$

2332 Clement Street (near 24th)
San Francisco
Telephone: (415) 386-2335
Cuisine: Cantonese and Mandarin

Hours:
    11:30 A.M.–10:00 P.M., Tuesday–Sunday

Credit cards: BA, MC

Patrons can choose from a wide variety of both Cantonese and Mandarin dishes at China West. If you like culinary surprises, tell the waiter how much you want to spend and leave your dinner to the cook. He will create a delicious meal based on the availability of fresh produce. The price for this dinner should be less than if you ordered dishes from the à la carte menu.

This family-style restaurant has a pleasantly decorated, comfortable interior. The service is good and the portions are generous considering the reasonable prices.

Specialties

Mandarin Spareribs
China West's Beef Supreme: Marinated beef stir-fried in a special sauce.
Fillet of Cod with Orange Sauce: Deep-fried cod served with orange sauce.
Deluxe Seafood Plate: Shrimp, abalone, and scallops.
Fish Balls Imperial: Fish balls with mixed vegetables.

MENU #1

Potstickers

China West's Beef Supreme

Deluxe Seafood Plate

Cantonese Fried Chicken

Mongolian Lamb *or* Beef

Steamed Rice

MENU #2

Velvet Chicken Corn Soup (chicken meat, corn, egg drop in thickened broth)

Fillet of Cod with Orange Sauce

Chicken with Vegetables

Mandarin Spareribs

Deep-fried Su Mi

Steamed Rice

MENU #3

Pressed Mandarin Duck

Beef Steak with Tender Greens

Cantonese Chicken Salad

Mu Shu Pork

Fish Balls Imperial

Steamed Rice

EASTERN BAKERY $

720 Grant Avenue
San Francisco
Telephone: (415) 982-5157
Cuisine: Cantonese and American

Hours:
    8:00 A.M.–7:00 P.M., daily

No credit cards

If you have finished a Chinese meal but are still hungry for dessert, stop by the Eastern Bakery, the oldest Chinese-American bakery in San Francisco's Chinatown. The Chinese sweets made here are renowned. Sample the sweet melon- or lotus-filled cakes with a thin, flaky, golden crust stamped with a red design. Or try the almond or sesame-seed cookies or the moon cakes, the later available from late August to early October and usually filled with fruit and nuts, coconut, or sweet winter melon.

"Most of our pastries are constructed of a kind of puff paste that has been rolled out in very thin layers," explains owner Mrs. Ling Lee. "Every pastry must be hand rolled and hand filled. The seam never shows." The carefully guarded family recipes used here have been passed on from generation to generation by observation and verbal instruction. "Nothing is written down," adds Mrs. Lee.

Drop in for coffee and a piece of fresh strawberry shortcake or lemon-crunch cake with whipped-cream frosting. They are very light and not too sweet. If you want a quick lunch, sit at the counter in the front or at one of the booths in the rear and order chow mein, chow fun, or fried rice. This place is often crowded, but the reasonable prices and delicious pastries make battling the crowds worthwhile.

EMPRESS OF CHINA $$$

838 Grant Avenue (near Clay)
San Francisco
Telephone: (415) 434-1345
Cuisine: Cantonese and Mandarin

Hours:
> 11:30 A.M.–3:00 P.M., 5:00 A.M.–11:00 P.M., Monday–Saturday
> 1:00 A.M.–11:00 P.M., Sunday

Credit cards: AE, BA, DC, Visa
Full bar
Reservations recommended

When you walk off the elevator onto the top floor of one of Chinatown's tallest buildings, the first thing you see is a large painting of the mythical Chinese empress of abundant harvest and prosperity. Antique ceremonial fans seem to surround you. Turn right and you enter the Dowager's Garden Court, filled with flowers. An impressive fifty-ton, octagonal, wooden pavilion, a replica of a garden palace in Peking, stands in the center. It was built by craftsmen in Taiwan, shipped to San Francisco, and reassembled at the Empress without the use of a single nail, its construction based on interlocking pieces of wood.

In the dining rooms are seven-foot-tall lanterns topped with peacock feathers (symbols of royalty), rare gilted carvings, and magnificent views through large bay windows. The Emperor's Chamber Room, reserved for private parties, has red silk-lined walls, arts objects of the Han era, and marble-topped teak tables. In the Golden Court Room, the frames on the wall mirrors are antique Peking shadow boxes, trimmed with blue kingfisher feathers. The atmosphere of the restaurant is one of serenity and elegance.

Among the fine dishes served here is flaming young quail. A whole quail is marinated in a special sauce, baked, and flamed with brandy at the table—truly superb.

The palacelike setting, panoramic city views, and excellent food will leave you with a very pleasant memory of Chinatown. When asked why he opened the Empress of China, director-owner H.K. Wong replied, "to share our cultural heritage, food, art, treasures, and friendship with all people."

Specialties

Silver Flower Scallop Soup: Delicious thick soup made with dried scallops, chicken, bamboo shoots, mushrooms, and egg drop.
Flaming Young Quail
Szechuan Spiced Beef
Mongolian Hundred Blossom Lamb: Lamb stir-fried with hoisin sauce.

Peking Duck (one day advance notice)
Sizzling Rice Soup
Smoked Tea Duck

MENU #1

Silver Flower Scallop Soup

Peking Rib Tidbits

Empress Chicken Salad

Sweet and Sour Rock Cod

Empress Beef

Steamed Rice

MENU #2

Potstickers

Hundred Blossom Lamb *or* Szechuan Spiced Beef

Empress Scallops

Mu Shu Pork

Lemon Chicken

Steamed Rice

MENU #3

Crab Meat Winter Melon Soup

Clam See Jup (clams stir-fried in black bean sauce) *or* See Jup Fillet of Rock Cod
   (fillet of rock cod stir-fried in black bean sauce)

Five Happiness Pork (slices of pork, onion, and celery stir-fried in plum sauce)

Steak Cubes with Chinese Greens

Steamed Rice

GOLDEN DRAGON NOODLE SHOP $

833 Washington Street (corner of Waverly)
San Francisco
Telephone: (415) 398-4550
Cuisine: Cantonese

Hours:
    7:00 A.M.–1:00 A.M., daily

No credit cards

You can peer in at the roast ducks, roast pork, and spareribs hanging in the window, while beyond them two or three cooks can be seen creating a fury in the kitchen. The deli and kitchen area extends out into the dining room of this very crowded, quick-order spot, renowned for its noodle and won ton dishes. The skin that encases the meat filling of the latter is so thin, it is almost transparent.

This is a favorite place for many locals for lunch or a midnight snack at bargain prices. You may want a side order of Chinese greens or broccoli with oyster sauce to accompany your meal. Service is minimal and little English is spoken, so if they don't understand you, point to what you want on the menu.

A caution: Don't get the rather small Golden Dragon Noodle Shop confused with the much larger Golden Dragon Restaurant across the street.

Specialties

Won Ton Soup: This is not the usual won ton soup. The filling has a great deal of shrimp and the broth is especially good.
Tender Greens in Oyster Sauce
Roast Duck
Barbecued Pork
Crispy Tender Pork: Barbecued whole pig with a very crisp skin; sliced to order. 脆皮乳豬

Congee Recommendations

Beef Porridge 牛肉粥

Pork Meatball Porridge 滑肉丸粥

Sampan Porridge: Shrimp, chicken, pork, abalone, and deep-fried peanuts.
Chicken Porridge

Rice Plate Recommendations

Shrimp with Tender Greens
Tender Chicken with Chinese Mushrooms
Beef with Egg: The egg in this dish is not "scrambled," but instead has a
  very smooth texture and delicious flavor,

Chow Mein and Chow Fun Recommendations

Beef Chow Fun
Beef with Tender Green Chow Mein
Chicken with Tender Green Chow Mein
Crab Meat with Straw Mushroom Lo Mein

GREAT EASTERN RESTAURANT $$

649 Jackson Street (near Kearny)
San Francisco
Telephone: (415) 397-0554
Cuisine: Cantonese

Hours:
    11:00 A.M.–3:00 A.M., Wednesday–Monday

Credit cards: MC, Visa
Full bar

This senior establishment has been patronized by Chinese families for many years. Stop by the doorway of the banquet room downstairs where families gather to celebrate a birthday or holiday. You will hear animated chatter as the diners discuss the dishes being served.

An especially attractive dish served here, one seldom found in other restaurants, is bok lui gwai chow, which translates as "one hundred birds in a nest." Slivers of taro root are pressed into a nest shape and deep-fried. The result is a crispy basket, or "nest," similar in texture to French-fried potatoes. Then a mixture of stir-fried shrimp, snow peas, bamboo shoots, celery, water chestnuts, and mushrooms are heaped into the taro-root nest. This stir-fry mixture represents the "one hundred birds" of the name. Another very good dish is the sweet and sour pork mixed with lychees, pineapple, green peppers, and onions, garnished with sesame seeds, and served attractively in a pineapple shell.

The dimly lit Great Eastern Restaurant, with its tasteful gold wallpaper and colorful red booths and chairs, is a very cozy dining spot.

Speciulties

Shrimp Mixture in a Taro Basket: Slivers of taro root are pressed into the shape of baskets and deep-fried, then filled with shrimp, snow peas, bamboo shoots, celery, water chestnuts, and mushrooms; listed on the Chinese menu only. 雀巢蝦仁

Sweet and Sour Pork
Crispy Chicken
Peking Duck (one day advance notice)
Steak Cubes with Chinese Greens
Minced Squab

Menu #1

Crispy Chicken (order a half chicken)

Steak Cubes with Chinese Greens

Sweet and Sour Pork

Steamed Whole Rock Cod

Steamed Rice

Menu #2

Diced Winter Melon Soup

Shrimp Mixture in a Taro Basket

Minced Squab

Chinese Greens in Oyster Sauce

Mongolian Beef

Steamed Rice

MENU #3

Stir-fried Lotus Root with Pork (listed on the Chinese menu only) 蓮藕小炒

Fillet of Rock Cod in Sweet and Sour Sauce

Squid with Chinese Greens *or* Beef with Chinese Greens

Cashew Nut Chicken

Steamed Rice

GREAT WALL RESTAURANT $$

815 Washington Street (near Grant)
San Francisco
Telephone: (415) 397-5826
Cuisine: Cantonese

Hours:
    11:00 A.M.–10:00 P.M., Wednesday–Monday

No credit cards

The original Great Wall Restaurant occupied part of the mezzanine floor in the same building that houses the Empress of China. It always bulged to capacity, with many more people waiting outside. In its new location, occupying two floors, it is still very busy, but waiting areas have been provided on each floor.

The restaurant specializes in family-style, clay-pot dinners, congee, noodles, and won tons, plus there is a good selection of à la carte Cantonese dishes that can be ordered for lunch or dinner. The food is tasty and the quality reliable, and though many of the waiters speak very little English, the service is good.

Specialties

King Du Spareribs 京都排骨
Clay-Pot Dishes
Crispy Chicken
Village-style Sautéed Clams: Clams stir-fried in black bean sauce.

MENU #1
Crispy Chicken (order a half chicken)
Prawns with Special Flavored Salt
Beef with Asparagus (seasonal) *or* Beef with Chinese Greens
King Du Spareribs
Steamed Rice

MENU #2
Black Bean Sauce Chicken
Bean Curd with Meats and Vegetables (in clay pot)
Village-style Sautéed Clams
Chinese Long Beans with Beef (seasonal) *or* Bok Choy with Beef
Steamed Rice

MENU #3
Shrimp with Tender Greens
Egg Rolls
Simmered Chicken with Onions (in clay pot)
Cashew Nut Chicken
Sum See in Oyster Sauce (sliced barbecued pork, bamboo shoots, bean sprouts, green onions, and chicken)
Steamed Rice

IMPERIAL PALACE $$$

919 Grant Avenue (near Jackson)
San Francisco
Telephone: (415) 982-4440
Cuisine: Cantonese

Hours:
    11:30 A.M.–1:00 A.M., Sunday–Thursday
    11:30 A.M.–2:00 A.M., Friday and Saturday

Credit cards: AE, CB, DC, MC, Visa
Full bar
Reservations recommended

Open the large, red doors of the Imperial Palace and stride across the lovely, plush carpeting. This sets the mood for the restaurant's beautiful interior of gold-papered walls, elegant place settings, roses in silver bud vases, and tall candelabrum. Elegance and luxury are evident everywhere.

The service is a match for the decor. Tuxedoed waiters bring the dishes out on serving carts and serve each guest individually.

All the dishes are expertly prepared and only the finest ingredients are used. New dishes from the Orient are regularly introduced here. Co-owner Joey Yuen and manager Tommie Toy both travel to the Far East often and return with recipes for the chef of the restaurant to master.

The Imperial Palace lives up to its motto: "Intimate dining fit for a connoisseur of Chinese cuisine."

Specialties

Peking Duck (one day advance notice)
Minced Squab Imperial
Flaming Quail: Barbecued quail, flamed with brandy at the table.
Lobster Imperial: Fresh, flavorful lobster meat quickly stir-fried in a
    special sauce.
Tossed Chicken Imperial (Cantonese chicken salad)

MENU #1

Shredded Scallop Soup

Tossed Chicken Imperial

Lobster in Black Bean Sauce

Braised Rock Cod

Mixed Fresh Vegetables

Steamed Rice

MENU #2

Minced Squab Imperial

Crab Meat Puff (deep-fried puffs with crab stuffing)

Barbecued Lamb

Chow Sam Ding (diced chicken, prawns, barbecued pork, bamboo shoots, and
water chestnuts in a spicy Szechuan sauce)

Steamed Rice

MENU #3

Peking Beef (hearty chunks of tenderloin beef cooked Peking style)

Straw Mushrooms with Oyster Sauce

Spiced Rock Cod (whole rock cod steamed in a spicy black bean sauce)

Sweet and Sour Pork

Prawns in Curry Sauce *or* Prawns Imperial (large prawns with button
mushrooms, snow peas, and Chinese ham)

Steamed Rice

JACKSON CAFE $

640 Jackson Street (near Kearny)
San Francisco
Telephone: (415) 986-9717 or 982-2409
Cuisine: Cantonese and American

Hours:
11:00 A.M.–10.00 P.M., daily

No credit cards

The Jackson Cafe is just that—a cafe! It is a favorite with the Chinese
because it has good food at very reasonable prices and because it serves
both Chinese and American cuisine.

The American entrées change daily and are listed on a menu attached to the regular bill of fare. A typical one is rib steak accompanied with soup, fresh rolls, and dessert. The steak is pan-fried in a wok, a cooking method that gives it an indescribably good flavor.

The Chinese house specialty is clams stir-fried with garlic sauce, a dish the adventurous diner will definitely not want to miss.

Specialties

Steamed Clams: Clams stir-fried in garlic sauce.
Steamed Rock Cod
Fried Chicken
Rice Casserole: Chicken, beef, shrimp or Chinese sausage with chicken.
Tender Greens with Beef

MENU #1

Steamed Clams

Tender Greens with Beef *or* Asparagus Beef

Chinese Mushroom Chicken

Spareribs with Black Bean Sauce

Steamed Rice

MENU #2

Fried Chicken (order a half chicken)

Ginger Beef

Shrimp with Black Bean Sauce

Chinese Sausage with Chicken Rice

MENU #3

Steamed Rock Cod

Tomato Beef

Paper-wrapped Chicken

Snow Peas Beef

Oyster Sauce with Tender Greens

Steamed Rice

JUNMAE GUEY $

1222 Stockton Street (near Broadway)
San Francisco
Telephone: (415) 433-3981
Cuisine: Cantonese

Hours:
    8:00 A.M.–6:00 P.M., Thursday–Tuesday

No credit cards

Through the front window of Junmae Guey one can see roast ducks, rock salt and soy sauce chickens, barbecued spareribs—all of which are deliciously prepared on the premises. This family-style delicatessen, known for its homemade noodles and won tons, is a good place for lunch or a snack. Though usually crowded at the noon hour, once you are seated service is fast. Order a plate of any one of the prepared meats as part of your lunch and don't resist the temptation to "take out" an order for dinner that same evening.

Specialties

Won Ton Soup: This is not the usual won ton soup. The filling has a great
    deal of shrimp and the broth is especially good.
Won Ton Noodle Soup
Roast Duck
Barbecued Pork
Barbecued Spareribs
Junmae Guey Pan-fried Noodles: Chicken, shrimp, barbecued pork, and
    mixed vegetables with noodles.
Sun See Chow Mein: Chicken, barbecued pork, bamboo shoots, and bean
    sprouts with noodles.

Congee Recommendations

Chicken Congee
Beef Congee
Sliced Fresh Fish Congee
Sliced Fresh Fish and Meatball Congee

Chow Mein and Rice Noodle Recommendations

Junmae Guey Pan-fried Noodles
Rice Noodle with Beef
Beef and Tomato Chow Mein
Sam See Chow Mein
Singapore Chow Rice Noodles (spicy)

Rice Plate Recommendations

Black Bean Sauce Spareribs with Rice
Beef and Tender Greens with Rice
Scrambled Egg and Beef with Rice: The egg in this dish is not really
    "scrambled," but instead has a very smooth texture and delicious flavor,
Chicken and Tender Greens with Rice
Soy Sauce Chicken with Rice

Special Plate Recommendations

Chicken with Greens
Shrimp with Tender Greens
Beef with Ginger in Oyster Sauce
Tender Greens in Oyster Sauce (ideal side dish with any of the prepared
    meats)

KAM LOK RESTAURANT $$

834 Washington Street (near Grant)
San Francisco
Telephone: (415) 421-8102
Cuisine: Cantonese

Hours:
    11:00 A.M.–midnight, daily

No credit cards

Just push open the glass doors and walk down the steps into Kam Lok
Restaurant. During the dinner hours, there is usually a waiting line at this
eatery. The decor is spartan, and it's rather noisy and crowded, but the

food is absolutely delicious. The reason Kam Lok is so popular is because it offers home-style cooking at its best at plain prices. Rather than going home to cook, many locals just eat out at Kam Lok.

Notice the glass tank filled with large fish near the kitchen. These fish are the specialty here. Called soong yeu, they are available year round, but are most plentiful during the winter. Hot oil and soy sauce are poured over the steamed fish, which is then garnished with green onions and slivers of ginger—delicate in flavor and very delicious. This type of fish does, however, have lots of bones. Order rock cod if you prefer a less bony fish, or one of the many other seafood dishes, all judiciously prepared here. Clay-pot casseroles are also popular with many of the patrons, and the won tons, rice plates, and noodles are lunch-time favorites.

There is a large selection of Cantonese dishes on the English menu, plus more on the three Chinese-menu pages. Many of the dishes that appear on the latter are favorites with the older Chinese, and we have included some of them in our list of specialties.

Specialties (listed on Chinese menu only)

Shredded Beef Strips: Marinated shredded beef stir-fried in special sauce, served without gravy. 干炒牛肉絲

Chicken (in clay pot) 啫啫鷄煲

Bean Cakes with Assorted Meats (in clay pot) 東江豆腐煲

Bean Cakes with Fish Balls (in clay pot) 魚蛋豆腐煲

King Du Spareribs 京都排骨

Double Mushrooms with Fresh Scallops 雙菇帶子

Sam See with Mixed Chinese Greens: Chicken, barbecued pork, and bamboo shoots with mixed Chinese vegetables. 翡翠炒三絲

Menu #1

Watercress and Pork Soup

Chinese Broccoli with Steak Cubes

Double Mushrooms with Fresh Scallops

Chicken (in clay pot)

Crab in Black Bean Sauce (seasonal) *or* King Du Spareribs

Steamed Rice

Menu #2

Pan-fried Prawns with Flavored Salt 椒鹽蝦

Deep-fried Stuffed Bean Cake (stuffed with fish paste and pork)

Shredded Beef Strips

Sam See with Mixed Chinese Greens

Bean Cakes and Fish Balls (in clay pot)

Steamed Rice

Menu #3

Clams in Black Bean Sauce *or* Shrimp in Black Bean Sauce

Stir-fried Chinese Greens

Fried Chicken Wings

Ginger Beef

Chinese Mushroom Chicken

Steamed Rice

KING WAH $$

852 Clement Street (corner of 10th)
San Francisco
Telephone: (415) 752-4900
Cuisine: Cantonese and Mandarin

Hours:
    11:30 A.M.–9:30 P.M., daily

Credit cards: MC, Visa
Full bar

Such delights as crackling shrimp, flaming lamb, and ginger pineapple duck are but a few of the creations at King Wah. Master chef-owner Cheung Leung has cooked at both the Imperial Palace and Shang Yeun restaurants and was head instructor at the cooking school sponsored by the Six Companies in Chinatown. To insure that only the finest ingredients are used in his restaurant, Mr. Leung insists on shopping for them himself.

King Wah is spacious, carpeted, and comfortable, and the friendly waiters move swiftly and efficiently to keep diners happy. Considering the excellent food, generous servings, pleasant surroundings, and attentive service, the prices are very moderate.

Specialties

Crispy Chicken　脆皮鷄

Clams in Spicy Black Bean Sauce　鼓汁炒大蜆

Fish Balls with Vegetables　爽滑荣魚丸

King Du Spareribs　京都排骨

Mongolian Lamb

MENU #1

Diced Winter Melon Soup

King Wah Chicken (chicken legs pan-fried with ginger, onions, and a special mushroom sauce)

Beef with Asparagus (seasonal) *or* Oyster Sauce Beef

Chinese Greens in Oyster Sauce

Crackling Shrimp (six shrimp deep-fried in rice paper)

Steamed Rice

MENU #2

King Du Spareribs

Clams in Spicy Black Bean Sauce

Crystal Prawns

Crispy Chicken (order a half chicken)

Mushrooms with Oyster Sauce

Steamed Rice

MENU #3

Mongolian Lamb

Almond Pressed Duck

Fish Balls with Vegetables

Asparagus with Black Bean Sauce (seasonal) *or* Mu Shu Pork

Steamed Rice

KUM MOON $$

2109 Clement Street (near 21st)
San Francisco
Telephone: (415) 221-5656
Cuisine: Cantonese and Mandarin

Hours:
    11:00 A.M.–9:30 P.M., Wednesday–Monday

Credit cards: BA, Visa

    This neighborhood eating spot is an emporium of surprises—delicious pastries, diem sum lunches, clay-pot specialties, and a large Cantonese and Mandarin menu. Most of the food here is delicious, well prepared, and very authentic, and the place is always busy, popular for lunch, dinner, coffee breaks, and snacks.
    If you are at Kum Moon for lunch, service is prompt and efficient. Order what the natives enjoy, a bowl of won ton soup and a plate of noodles, and share it between two people. (Of course, request an extra plate and soup bowl.)
    The original Kum Moon, located on Geary Boulevard was so popular as to necessitate a move to the present larger location. The new address maintains the same fine caliber food that the Geary Street location served.

Specialties

Clams Sautéed in Black Bean Sauce
Mu Shu Pork
Chinese Broccoli with Oyster Sauce
Mongolian Lamb *or* Beef
Lemon Sweet and Sour Chicken: Deep-fried chicken with lemon sauce.
Spareribs with Pineapple: Deep-fried spareribs with pineapple and sweet
   and sour sauce.
Clay-Pot Dishes

Lunch Menu Recommendations

Pork Chow Mein *or* Chow Fun
Beef with Tomato Chow Mein
Tomato Beef with Curry Chow Mein
Boneless Chicken with Vegetable Chow Mein *or* Chow Fun

Gum-Lo Fried Won Ton: Won ton in sweet and sour sauce with mixed meat.

Wor Won Ton Soup

Hong Tao Yee Won Ton

Sing Chow Fried Rice Noodles: Thin rice noodles prepared with or without curry.

Diem Sum Trays

MENU #1 (Mandarin)

Potstickers

Sizzling Rice Soup *or* Hot and Sour Soup

Mongolian Beef or Lamb

Shelled Prawns with Red Pepper

Mu Shu Pork

Deep-fried Chicken with Garlic Sauce

Steamed Rice

MENU #2 (Cantonese)

Winter Melon Crab Meat Soup

Chinese Broccoli *or* Tender Chinese Greens

Clams Sautéed in Black Bean Sauce

Beef under Snow

Spareribs with Pineapple

Cherry Blossom Vegetable in Scrambled Eggs (barbecued pork, bean sprouts, bamboo shoots, celery, yellow onion in eggs)

Steamed Rice

MENU #3 (Cantonese)

Scallops in Scrambled Egg Soup

Prawns Sauté with Cashew Nuts

Beef with Snow Peas

Lemon Sweet and Sour Chicken

Braised Duck with Mixed Meat (order a half duck)

Steamed Rice

THE MANDARIN $$$

900 North Point, Ghirardelli Square
San Francisco
Telephone: (415) 673-8812
Cuisine: Mandarin

Hours:
    noon–11:30 P.M., Monday–Friday
    12:30 P.M.–11.30 P.M., Saturday and Sunday

Credit cards: AE, BA, CB, DC, MC, Visa
Full bar
Reservations advised
Parking lot downstairs

The enticing aromas you smell in the air at Ghirardelli Square are most likely from The Mandarin, one of the most beautiful Chinese restaurants in San Francisco. The gastronomic accomplishments that come from the kitchen are memorable. Attractive presentations of each dish and excellent service are standard here. Many of the specialties on the menu were created by the restaurant's famous owner, Cecilia Chiang, and such culinary delights as beggar's chicken, smoked tea duck, minced squab, and Mongolian lamb are just a few of the savory dishes that must be tried.

Madame Chiang was born into the elite class of pre-revolutionary China. Throughout her early years she was exposed to the best things in life, including the finest Chinese cuisine. She learned to appreciate fine food from her mother, who was an excellent cook. When Madame Chiang married and moved to Tokyo, she yearned for the excellent foods of her childhood. Good, sophisticated Chinese food was non-existent in Tokyo in those days, so she opened a restaurant.

"I clearly remembered how the food should taste, so I kept perfecting each dish," recalls Madame Chiang. While visiting a sister in San Francisco in 1961, she decided to open a small restaurant on Polk Street. This was the first Mandarin restaurant in San Francisco, and it was slow in becoming established because northern Chinese food was virtually unknown here. Once word spread of the excellent fare, however, there were waiting lines, and today, in its present spacious setting, The Mandarin has a large, dedicated following.

The building that houses the restaurant withstood the big earthquake and fire in 1906, and the original brick and wood blend beautifully with the elegant surroundings. The rooms are divided with wooden screens and the walls are graced with antique scrolls, paintings, and embroidery. Large wooden pillars and beams hold up the high, grass-lined ceiling. The hardwood floors are covered with beautiful Oriental carpets.

The Mandarin resembles an elegant, comfortable house in old China, and Cecilia Chiang runs her restaurant as a great lady would run her home. If she isn't in Beverly Hills supervising her other restaurant, she does the marketing and consults with the chef daily, and is often on hand to greet diners.

No shortcut methods in food preparation are used. For example, the beggar's chicken is rubbed on the outside with rice wine and five-spice powder, stuffed with ham, water chestnuts, mushrooms, and bamboo shoots, encased in clay, and cooked slowly in the oven. When the clay case is cracked open, the aroma is unforgettable.

Dining at The Mandarin is a wonderful experience. Though very expensive, it is, in our opinion, well worth the cost. Madame Chiang or manager Lisan Chien will assist you by phone in planning a special dinner.

Specialties

Chiao-Tzu: Small dumpling turnovers filled with a delicate meat stuffing, grilled crisp on one side, and served with vinegar and hot pepper oil.
Mongolian Lamb *or* Beef: Slices of tenderloin of lamb or beef stir-fried with scallions, *or* grilled quickly over the Mongolian fire pit; served in hot Mandarin buns.
Prawns à la Szechuan: Tender young prawns in a spicy, flavorful, hot red sauce.
Mu Shu Pork
Beggar's Chicken: A fowl, finely flavored, encased in clay, and baked.
Smoked Tea Duck

MENU #1

Sizzling Rice Soup

Chiao-Tzu

Mongolian Lamb *or* Beef

Mandarin Sweet and Sour Fish

Snow Peas with Mushrooms and Water Chestnuts

Steamed Rice

Menu #2

Hot and Sour Soup

Smoked Tea Duck (order a half duck)

Shrimp with Snow Peas

Peking Sweet and Sour Pork

Bon Bon Chi (salad of torn chicken and julienne-cut cucumber with red pepper
 and sesame seeds)

Steamed Rice

Menu #3

Beggar's Chicken

Mu Shu Pork

Prawns à la Szechuan

Baby Corn with Mushrooms

Steamed Rice

MIKE'S CHINESE CUISINE $$

5145 Geary Boulevard (near 15th)
San Francisco
Telephone: (415) 752-0120
Cuisine: Cantonese

Hours:
    4:30 P.M–10:00 P.M., Wednesday–Monday

Credit cards: MC, Visa
Full bar

Though the fare here is strictly Cantonese, Mike creates the traditional dishes with imagination and flair. The results are irresistible delights
that are consistently delicious, since Mike is always supervising in the
kitchen during dinner hours. He is an expert in blending textures, flavors,
and seasonings, and the delicate, mildly seasoned dishes will linger in your

mind until you return here again. The menu selection is somewhat brief by
Chinese restaurant standards, but almost every entrée is a masterpiece.

This small family-style, family-run restaurant is quickly being discovered, even though it's far from Chinatown. Cozy surroundings, distinctive food, and good service at moderate prices make this spot a must.

Specialties

Stir-fried Clams: Clams sautéed in black bean sauce.
Chicken with Black Beans and Bell Pepper: A spicy dish not listed on the
  menu.
Egg Rolls
Mongolian Beef
West Lake Duck (Stewed Duck) (order one day in advance) 西湖鴨
Guo Jee Op (Barley Duck) (order one day in advance) 菓子鴨

Menu #1
Butterfly Prawns
Diced Winter Melon Soup
Shredded Barbecued Chicken Salad
Mongolian Beef
Stir-fried Clams
Steamed Rice

Menu #2
Spring Egg Rolls
Beef with Chinese Greens
Crab with Black Bean Sauce (seasonal) *or* Crystal Shrimp
Chicken with Black Beans and Bell Pepper
Steamed Rice

Menu #3
Sweet and Sour Rock Cod Fillet *or* Sweet and Sour Whole Rock Cod
Spring Egg Rolls

Chicken with Mushrooms and Chinese Greens

Oyster Sauce Beef

Pan-fried Prawns in Shell

Steamed Rice

OCEAN GARDEN RESTAURANT $

735 Jackson Street
San Francisco
Telephone: (415) 421-9129
Cuisine: Cantonese

Hours:
11:30 A.M.–1:00 A.M., daily

No credit cards

When you look through the windows of Ocean Garden Restaurant, you may say to yourself, "What a small eating place." Look beyond the eating area into the kitchen and you can see several cooks working over their woks, and waiters, laden with hot dishes, running out of the kitchen and up the stairs. Yes, there is a second floor at Ocean Garden, but it is only slightly larger than the first.

A varied selection of seafood is on the menu and all of the dishes are excellent. The ingredients blend so well in the sautéed clams with black bean sauce that you may not be able to detect exactly what the seasonings are, only that they are superb. The prawns here are stir-fried to a perfect golden brown. Five seconds more would toughen them. The stir-fried scallops with Chinese greens illustrates the knack the cooks have with seafood and vegetable combinations. The scallops are juicy and soft, while the greens are shiny and crunchy. For vegetarians, there are at least two selections on the menu, plus there are a number of clay-pot dishes for all diners.

Over the last few years, four or five restaurants have opened and closed in this same location. When Ocean Garden opened, however, it became an instant hit. The generous servings of well-prepared food at reasonable prices and the quick service have insured its success.

Specialties

West Lake Beef Soup: A thick soup with seasoned, minced beef, coriander, and egg drop.
Dried Scallop with Egg Flower Soup
Chicken in Clay Pot: Pieces of seasoned chicken simmered in a delicious sauce.
Scallops and Shrimp with Chinese Greens
Salt-baked Chicken: This is a popular dish in Hong Kong; a special recipe with unparalleled taste and tenderness.

MENU #1

West Lake Beef Soup

Steak Cubes

Chicken with Plum Sauce

Sautéed Clams with Black Bean Sauce

Double Kinds of Vegetables with Oyster Sauce (Chinese broccoli and Chinese greens)

Steamed Rice

MENU #2

Chicken in Clay Pot

Dried Scallop with Egg Flower Soup

Kung Pao Chicken

Steamed Whole Rock Cod *or* Shrimp with Black Bean Sauce

Dry-fried Prawns

Steamed Rice

MENU #3

Spareribs with Flavored Salt　椒鹽排骨

Salt-baked Chicken (order a half chicken)

Beef with Tender Greens

Scallops and Shrimp with Greens

Double Mushrooms with Oyster Sauce

Steamed Rice

THE POT STICKER $$

150 Waverly Place (near Washington)
San Francisco
Telephone: (415) 397-9985
Cuisine: Mandarin

Hours:
   11:30 A.M.–10:00 P.M., daily

Credit cards: MC, Visa

   One of the best places to eat northern-style food in Chinatown, The Pot Sticker, with its modern decor and hanging plants, is a very popular spot. The large front window looks out onto Waverly Place, a narrow thoroughfare that will remind you of eating in a restaurant on a small, crowded street in the Far East.
   For those living on the peninsula, you can visit the original Pot Sticker at 3708 South El Camino Real in San Mateo (page 145).

Specialties

Szechuan Crispy Fish: Deep-fried whole fish with finely chopped ginger, onions, and hot bean sauce.
Orange Spareribs: Barbecued spareribs with orange sauce.
Hunan Crispy Chicken: Deep-fried pieces of chicken topped with hot bean sauce.
Mongolian Beef

MENU #1
Sizzling Rice Soup

Potstickers

Hunan Beef

Hunan Crispy Chicken (order a half chicken)

Straw Mushrooms and Baby Corn or Assorted Vegetables

Steamed Rice

MENU #2

Hot and Sour Soup

Mongolian Beef

Orange Spareribs

Szechuan Crispy Fish *or* Velvet Chicken

Hot Bean Curd (diced bean cake, ground pork, peas, and mushrooms in a spicy
bean sauce)

Steamed Rice

MENU #3

Family Deluxe (mainly seafood, plus chicken, bamboo shoots, and mushrooms)
or Sizzling Rice Shrimp

Assorted Vegetables

Green Onion Beef

Velvet Chicken

Steamed Rice

RUBY PALACE $$

631 Kearny Street (near Washington)
San Francisco
Telephone: (415) 433-3196
Cuisine: Cantonese and Mandarin

Hours:
11:30 A.M.–3:00 P.M., 5:00 P.M.–10:00 P.M., Monday–Friday
11:00 A.M.–10:00 P.M., Saturday and Sunday

Credit cards: BA, DC, MC
Full bar
Reservations recommended on weekends

This eating spot is extremely popular with business people from the
Financial District. They come to sip a cocktail and relax in the spacious,
clean, carpeted, air-conditioned rooms while waiting for a table.

Ruby Palace is one of the few places in Chinatown where you can get a delicious luncheon plate that includes soup, entrée over rice, fresh fruit, and tea for a reasonable price. The entrée may be almond chicken, Mandarin beef, or sweet and sour pork. If you prefer a diem sum lunch, just head upstairs. During the evening hours, the locals can be seen ordering many of their favorite dishes here, such as fresh scallops in bean sauce and whole braised fish. If you want a special meal for a group, mention a price to the manager and see what the kitchen can create for you. The service here is prompt and the waiters are courteous.

Specialties

Sweet and Sour Spareribs, Peking Style
General Tsuo's Chicken: Cubes of chicken prepared with a hot-and-sour wine sauce.
Chicken Breasts with Egg White Sauce
Mandarin Crispy Duck
Clay-Pot Dishes

Menu #1

Three Ingredient Soup (sliced abalone, scallops, and shrimp in chicken broth)

Kung Pao Chicken

Cantonese Crab (seasonal) *or* Fish Fillet in Black Bean Sauce

Mu Shu Pork

Steamed Rice

Menu #2

Szechuan Cold Chicken (spicy)

Chicken Breasts with Egg Sauce

Mandarin Beef (beef and mixed vegetables in a spicy sauce)

Sweet and Sour Spareribs, Peking Style

Steamed Rice

Menu #3

Chungking Beef (marinated beef with celery and water chestnuts in hot sauce)
    or Broccoli Beef

Mixed Seafood in Casserole

Szechuan-style Eggplant (stir-fried eggplant with hot sauce) *or* Szechuan-style
    String Beans (string beans stir-fried with spicy, minced pork)

Steamed Rice

SONG HAY $$

650 Jackson Street (near Grant)
San Francisco
Telephone: (415) 982-3344
Cuisine: Cantonese

Hours:
    10:00 A.M.–10:00 P.M., daily

No credit cards

If you want to get away from the tourist area and venture to a place
the locals patronize, walk down Jackson Street from Grant Avenue to
Song Hay. It is a bit more spacious and less crowded than many of the
eating places closer to Grant, and it offers quality home-style cooking. A
delicious soup of the day, better than that served at most places, is usually
included with the meal if two or more items are ordered from the menu.

All of the dishes are prepared with the diner's value in mind. For example, if beef with beans is ordered, you needn't worry that the dish will
arrive with an abundance of beans, some onions for filler, and only a little
meat. The cook will be sure to include a healthy-sized portion of meat
with the vegetables. Most everything is well prepared here, with a special
nod to the very good clay-pot dishes.

Specialties

Steak Cubes

Crab with Ginger and Black Bean Sauce (seasonal)

Chicken in Clay Pot   啫啫鷄煲

Bean Cakes with Assorted Meats in Clay Pot   八珍豆腐煲

Spiced Beef in Oyster Sauce: Beef and mixed vegetables stir-fried in a
    spiced oyster sauce.

MENU #1

Beef under Snow
Crab with Ginger and Black Bean Sauce *or* Prawns with Black Bean Sauce
Chicken in Clay Pot
Barbecued Pork with Baby Corn
Steamed Rice

MENU #2

Chinese-style Fried Chicken
Tender Greens with Beef
Bean Cakes with Assorted Meats in Clay Pot
Prawns with Cashew Nuts
Steamed Rice

MENU #3

Spiced Beef in Oyster Sauce
Peking Spareribs　京都排骨
Almond Chicken Ding
Prawns with Lobster Sauce
Steamed Rice

SUN HUNG HEUNG $$

744 Washington Street (near Kearny)
San Francisco
Telephone: (415) 982-2319
Cuisine: Cantonese

Hours:
　　11:30 A.M.–midnight, Wednesday–Monday

Credit cards: BA, MC
Full bar
Reservations needed for six or more

This restaurant, the oldest in Chinatown, has been a favorite of both natives and visitors for over fifty years. The menu is quite extensive, with a wide variety of Cantonese dishes. To truly appreciate the culinary accomplishments of this fine restaurant, order the stuffed crab legs, taro duck, or shark's fin soup—the latter the best in town! The stuffed chicken wings are a truly remarkable achievement. The wings are boned and a mixture of chopped pork, shrimp, and mushrooms is stuffed into the skins until they are stretched to three times their original size. The wings are then deep-fried to a golden brown, sliced, and served with brown gravy. The price for this fantastic creation is so low, you won't believe it.

If it looks busy on the first floor, don't fret. There is a large dining room upstairs, with semiprivate booths and tables covered with linen cloths. Sun Hung Heung has been run by the same family in the same location since 1919, and has always provided reliable food and service.

Specialties

Shark's Fin Soup
Fried Stuffed Chicken Wings: Boned wings stuffed with pork, chicken
    meat, mushrooms, and water chestnuts; served with a delicious gravy.
Cantonese Chicken Salad
Raw Fish Salad
Beef under Snow

Menu #1

Clams Sautéed in Black Bean Sauce

Mongolian Beef

Fried Stuffed Chicken Wings

Steamed Rock Cod *or* Shelled Prawns with Vegetables

Steamed Rice

Menu #2

Cantonese Chicken Salad

Snow Peas with Black Mushrooms

Asparagus with Black Bean Sauce (seasonal) *or* Stir-fried Chinese Greens

Beef under Snow

Grilled Prawns with Bacon (butterfly prawns)

Steamed Rice

MENU #3

Cracked Crab (seasonal; with curry, black bean, or ginger and green onion sauce)
    or Prawns with Lobster Sauce

Chicken with Black Mushrooms

Chinese Greens with Ginger

Stir-fried Chinese-style Steak

Roast Duck

Steamed Rice

SUN TAI SAM YUEN $

622 Jackson Street (near Kearny)
San Francisco
Telephone: (415) 982-2844
Cuisine: Cantonese and American

Hours:
    11:00 A.M.–11:00 P.M., daily

No credit cards

Generations of San Francisco residents know they can get good, economically priced Chinese and American food at Sun Tai Sam Yuen, one of the oldest restaurants in Chinatown. All types of people can be seen here, from sophisticated business folks to adventurous seniors.

This is simple, utilitarian dining. The decor is plain and the service is minimal, but just about everything on the menu is tasty and reliable, and the prices are very low considering the quality of food.

Sit at the counter or in one of the pink booths. If there are five or more in your party, however, go straight back and down a few steps to the banquet room.

Specialties

Dried Scallop Soup
Choy Yuen Chicken: Chinese greens with marinated chicken.

Garlic Sauce Clams: Stir-fried clams with ginger and garlic sauce.
Chinese-style Fried Chicken
Subgum Scallops: Scallops stir-fried with mushrooms, bamboo shoots, carrots, celery, and snow peas.

MENU #1

Dried Scallop Soup

Choy Yuen Beef *or* Choy Yuen Chicken

Chinese-style Fried Chicken (order a half chicken)

Chinese Peas with Shrimp

Subgum Scallops

Steamed Rice

MENU #2

Winter Melon Soup

Garlic Sauce Clams

Almond Duck *or* Lychee Chicken (deep-fried chicken pieces with lychees in sweet and sour sauce)

Shrimp with Lobster Sauce

Mushroom Abalone

Steamed Rice

MENU #3

Beef with Oyster Sauce

Chinese Peas Chicken

Clams in Black Bean Sauce

Scallops with Choy Yuen

Abalone in Oyster Sauce

Steamed Rice

TONG KEE #1 $

854 Washington Street (near Stockton)
Telephone: (415) 982-0936 or 982-0937

Hours:
    10:30 A.M.–1:00 A.M., daily

TONG KEE #2

1365 Stockton Street (corner of Vallejo)
Telephone: (415) 956-8336

Hours:
    10:30 A.M.–9:00 P.M., daily

TONG KEE #3

710 Kearny Street (near Washington)
Telephone: (415) 982-5341 or 982-5342

Hours:
    10:30 A.M.–9:00 P.M., daily

San Francisco
Cuisine: Cantonese

No credit cards

    The small, unpretentious Tong Kee restaurant on Washington Street became so popular for its won ton soup and noodle dishes that in two years' time another larger and more spacious establishment was opened on Stockton. Mrs. Chao, the proprietor, owned a noodle and won ton restaurant in Hong Kong before coming to San Francisco and opening her first place here.

Drop in at Tong Kee #1 for a quick snack or light lunch and order any of the noodle or won ton dishes. The noodles and won ton skins are made on the premises. Tong Kee #2 is more spacious and the menu is more extensive than at the original location. It features all of the same items, as well as a number of traditional dishes, such as pork tripe, pig's feet in black vinegar sauce, and clay-pot favorites. Just a few doors away from the Holiday Inn, right across the street from Portsmouth Square, is Tong Kee #3, serving the same good food found at the other branches.

Specialties

Won Ton Soup

Beef Stew Won Ton Soup　牛腩雲吞

Beef Stew Won Ton and Noodle Soup　牛腩雲吞麵
Deep-fried Stuffed Bean Cakes: Bean cake stuffed with fish paste.
Clay-Pot Dishes
Crispy Chicken

MENU #1

Stir-fried clams

Bean Cake with Vegetables (in clay pot)

Chicken in Clay Pot

Crispy Chicken

Steak with Tender Greens

Steamed Rice

MENU #2

Abalone with Oyster Sauce

Almond Chicken Ding

Bean Cake with Eight Precious Ingredients (in clay pot)

Prawns with Ginger and Green Onion (in clay pot)

Steamed Rice

Menu #3

Egg Flower Soup

Prawns with Black Bean Sauce and Green Pepper

Fried Chicken Wings

Beef with Chinese Greens

Bean Cake with Eight Precious Ingredients (in clay pot)

Steamed Rice

VEGI FOOD $$

1820 Clement Street
San Francisco
Telephone: (415) 387-8111
Cuisine: Vegetarian Cantonese and Mandarin

Hours:
> 11:30 A.M.–3:00 P.M., 5:00 P.M.–9:00 P.M., Tuesday–Friday
> 11:30 A.M.–9:00 P.M., Saturday and Sunday

No credit cards

"I opened my restaurant to serve the Buddhist people because there were few choices of places to dine in the Bay Area. I also wanted to expand the Buddhist philosophy to encourage people not to kill any kind of life," comments David Chan, owner of the Vegi restaurant. When Vegi Food, San Francisco's first Chinese vegetarian restaurant, opened, it was an instant success. Using no onions, eggs, garlic, or monosodium glutamate, Mr. Chan is ingenious in combining ingredients and spices to bring out the natural flavors of food. The restaurant features fresh vegetable dishes, combined with high-protein ingredients such as gluten wheat or soy bean products. Foods are often garnished with such earthy ingredients as fungus, mushrooms, and nuts.

To ensure controllable and repeatable flavors, only the finest ingredients are used. The preparation methods are often time-consuming and exhausting. For a basic soup stock, dried soy beans are soaked, and the resulting sprouts are boiled with the best quality black mushrooms; a soy bean paste is then added as the stock is simmered for many hours. Mr. Chan's Shark's Fin Soup tastes like the genuine thing.

We were pleased to discover how tasty the Fried Won Tons were without meat in the filling. Another delight was crunchy, crispy chunks of walnuts blended well in a sweet-sour sauce laden with fresh carrots, tomatoes, bell peppers, water chestnuts, and pineapple.

A larger Vegi Food restaurant has opened at 2083–85 Vine Street in Berkeley. Mr. Chan is now chef at the newest restaurant, while his wife, Irene, operates the San Francisco establishment. Both restaurants are immaculate and cheerful looking, with waiters trained to satisfy the many patrons who have come seeking delicious, nutritious, wholesome meals. They will even serve hot, steamed *brown* rice on request!

Specialties

Lo-Han Jai: Mixed vegetables deluxe
Fried Walnuts with Sweet and Sour Sauce
Mu Shu Vegetables with Pancakes
Braised Eggplant: Sliced, deep-fried, and mixed with tofu, mushrooms, carrots, celery, and black fungus.

Lunch Menu Recommendations

Lo-Hon Mixed Vegetable Chow Mein
Bean Curd in Black Bean Sauce Chow Mein: Sliced fried tofu and bell peppers, stir-fried with three kinds of mushrooms, bamboo shoots, fungus, and water chestnuts, mixed with black bean paste and served over pan-fried noodles.
Lo-Hon Noodle Soup

MENU #1
Potstickers

Corn Porridge with Vegetables

Black Mushroom and Green Chow Mein

Colorful Shredded Vegetables

Fried Walnuts with Sweet and Sour Sauce

Steamed Rice

MENU # 2

Fried Won Tons with Sweet and Sour Sauce

Sizzling Rice Soup

Stewed Mushrooms with Greens

Diced Mushrooms and Cashew Nuts

Fried Walnuts with Sweet and Sour Sauce

Steamed Rice

YET WAH $$

2140 Clement Street (corner of 23rd)
Telephone: (415) 387-8040

Hours:
    4:00 P.M.–11:00 P.M., daily

1829 Clement Street (near 19th)
Telephone: (415) 387-8056, 751-1231

Hours:
    11:30 A.M.–11:00 P.M., daily

5238 Diamond Heights Boulevard
Telephone: (415) 282-0788

Hours:
    4:00 P.M.–11:00 P.M., daily

Pier 39
Telephone: (415) 434-4430

Hours:
    11:30 A.M.–11:00 P.M., daily

San Francisco
Cuisine: Mandarin

Credit cards: AE, BA, DC, MC
Full bar except at 1801 Clement Street
Reservations recommended for six or more

Yet Wah is the fastest-growing Chinese-restaurant chain in the Bay Area. The master wizard behind the success is Bill Hoon Sing Chan. At sixteen, Mr. Chan was a kitchen helper in a large restaurant in his native China. He was so enthusiastic about the menial duties he performed in the kitchen, the boss kept assigning him to more difficult tasks. In two years' time, he was permitted to cook a few dishes, which delighted many of the patrons. After putting his culinary interests aside for a few years to study in Hong Kong, Mr. Chan began visiting relatives who owned Chinese restaurants in different parts of the world. He exchanged cooking ideas with them and experimented with different dishes. Then in 1969, he started a family-style, family-run restaurant at 1801 Clement Street in San Francisco, the original Yet Wah, now a prime rib house.

In those days, Mr. Chan could be seen creating new dishes in the kitchen, running out to the eating area to elicit his patrons' opinions of them, then hurrying back to the kitchen to prepare more dishes with the assistance of family members. The most popular dishes stayed on the menu, while the less favored ones were dropped. Today, Mr. Chan has a repertoire of over 250 dishes on the menu. New ones are still being added, but only fast enough to allow him to personally train each chef in his nine restaurants, most of whom are family members who have worked with Mr. Chan for many years.

The new dishes first appear on the menu at 2140 Clement, the largest of the chain and its headquarters. Don't form any opinions about it based on its rather garish exterior. On the inside, this restaurant is very modern, spacious, air-conditioned, and efficiently run by manager Bryant Medge and his well-trained staff. Mr. Medge stresses that the food is always fresh and that the "Yet Wah touch" is added to many traditional dishes. For example, the Yet Wah potstickers are simply out of this world.

The menu is essentially the same in all branches. The foods are fresh and cooked to order. The service is usually personable and prompt.

Specialties

Su Mi: Deep-fried meat-filled "ravioli"; among the best in town.
Potstickers
Sweet and Sour Fish

Butterfly Prawns
Mu Shu Pork
Deep-fried Squid
Smoked Tea Duck

MENU #1

Potstickers

Sizzling Rice Soup

Szechuan Spiced Beef (spicy)

Lemon Chicken

Kung Pao Prawns

Steamed Rice

MENU #2

Su Mi

Hot and Sour Soup

Mongolian Beef *or* Asparagus Beef with Black Bean Sauce (seasonal)

Kung Pao Chicken

Water Chestnuts with Pea Pods

Steamed Rice

MENU #3

Deep-fried Squid *or* Butterfly Prawns

Mu Shu Pork

Mongolian Lamb

Braised Whole Fish with Brown Bean Sauce

Smoked Tea Duck (order a half duck)

Steamed Rice

YUET LEE $

1300 Stockton Street (corner of Broadway)
San Francisco
Telephone: (415) 982-6020
Cuisine: Cantonese

Hours:
    11:00 A.M.–3:00 A.M., Wednesday–Monday

No credit cards

Located on the busy corner of Broadway and Stockton streets, this modest restaurant, with its arched cathedral-style windows, reminds us of a European bistro. The kitchen extends out into the dining area, and patrons can "people watch" through the windows from almost every table. The menu is written in Chinese on a huge blackboard in the center of the room and on two mirrors hung at opposite ends of it. (English menus are also available.) It is amazing what fine dishes this small restaurant can produce, and so quickly, too. A perfect place for a late-night repast.

Specialties

Tamale: Sweet rice, pork, chestnuts, peanuts, shrimp, and mushrooms; steamed in lotus leaves.
Fried Shrimp Cake
Steamed Chicken with Mushrooms: Seasoned chicken pieces combined with shredded red dates, mushrooms, lily flowers, and green onions.
Clay-Pot Dishes
Prawns with Flavored Salt and Green Pepper

Rice Plate Recommendations

Abalone with Chicken Rice
Chicken Rice
Prawns with Tender Greens Rice
Scrambled Egg with Shrimp
Sum See Rice: Sliced chicken, bamboo shoots, bean sprouts, and barbecued pork.

Beef with Tender Greens Rice
Young Chow Fried Rice: Barbecued pork, bean sprouts, yellow onion, green onions, peas, and egg.

Menu #1

Seafood with Bean Cake Soup

Tender Greens Sauté

Kung Pao Shrimp

Braised Chicken with Abalone

Sautéed Sliced Pork with Tender Greens

Steamed Rice

Menu #2

Stuffed Bean Cake with Variety Meats (in clay pot)

Sweet and Sour Pork

Green Pepper with Beef

Steamed Chicken with Mushrooms

Fried Shrimp Cake

Steamed Rice

Menu #3

Abalone and Chicken Wor Noodles (abalone and chicken in noodle soup)

Sautéed Crab with Black Bean Sauce (seasonal) *or* Sautéed Curry Crab (seasonal)

Sautéed Prawns with Tender Greens

Sum See Bean Sprouts (barbecued pork, bamboo shoots, mushrooms or celery, and bean sprouts)

Braised Chicken with Oyster Sauce

Steamed Rice

EAST BAY

BOK SEN $$

710 Webster Street
Oakland
Telephone: (415) 465-4001
Cuisine: Cantonese

Hours:
    11:30 A.M.–11:30 P.M., daily

Credit cards: MC, Visa
Full bar

Owner Jack Ong may have the best personality of any restaurateur in Oakland. As soon as he seated us, Mr. Ong motioned the waiter over to serve tea and present the menu. The cocktail waitress appeared moments later. After the cocktail orders were taken, the waiter arrived to take our dinner requests. What perfect synchronization of service! About halfway through the meal, Mr. Ong came by to be sure that the food and service were meeting with our approval.

This restaurant serves the two best Chinese sparerib dishes in town. One of our friends ate the Peking spareribs and commented, "An exquisite taste that cannot be described, but will linger in your mind until you return here again."

Bok Sen, with its comfortable, very modern decor, is a favorite dining spot for many residents in the East Bay.

Specialties

Fried Spareribs: Deep-fried spareribs with flavored salt.
Peking Spareribs
Steak Cubes Cantonese
Kubla Beef: Sliced tender beef sautéed with mixed Chinese vegetables.
West Lake Duck (order one day in advance)
Guo Jee Op (Barley Duck) (order one day in advance)

MENU #1

Bird's Nest Soup *or* Egg Flower Soup

Sweet and Sour Rock Cod Fillet

Peking Spareribs

Steak Cubes Cantonese

Crab in Black Bean Sauce (seasonal) *or* Shrimp Sautéed with Black and White
Mushrooms

Steamed Rice

MENU #2

Butterfly Prawns

Mushroom Chicken (sliced boneless chicken sautéed with mushrooms in oyster
sauce)

Fried Spareribs with Pepper Salt

Kubla Beef

Crab Foo Young

MENU #3

Peking Spareribs

Sweet Peas with Beef

Pineapple Chicken

Abalone in Oyster Sauce

Stir-fried Chinese Greens

Steamed Rice

CHINA PAVILION $$$

2050 Diamond Boulevard (at Concord)
Concord
Telephone: (415) 827-2212
Cuisine: Cantonese and Mandarin

Hours:
   11:30 A.M.–10:00 P.M., Monday–Friday
   4:00 P.M.–10:00 P.M., Saturday
   11:30 A.M.–10:00 P.M., Sunday

Credit cards: AE, MC, Visa
Full bar

From the outside, China Pavilion presents a regal appearance, inviting one to venture within and taste its gourmet delights. As you enter its portals, you find yourself in a majestic foyer that serves as the waiting area. Directly in front of the foyer is a miniature Oriental garden, with a stream winding its way down rocks in a sylvan setting. To the right is a tastefully appointed cocktail lounge, a warm and cozy area in which one may relax and await a table. The dining area is directly opposite the lounge. It is a spacious room, with a silk canopy suspended from the ceiling that adds much to the Oriental decor.

China Pavilion is owned and operated by Ping Ping Lee and her husband. As expressed in the welcoming note on the front of the menu, it is their "hope that they may bring some of the pleasures of Chinese dining from each province" to their customers.

The broad range of dishes offered, the warm, inviting ambience, and the attentive service from both owners and staff make the China Pavilion a truly memorable dining experience. A word of advice, though. The menu offers several dishes that require a twenty-four hour notice. The first-time diner is well advised to call ahead and inquire about these dishes. Placing the order in advance will avoid the disappointment of not being able to enjoy them. A Sunday buffet, which includes complimentary champagne, is also served.

Specialties

China Pavilion Appetizers: Fried prawns, skewered steak, paper-wrapped chicken, rumaki (chicken liver wrapped with bacon and deep-fried), barbecued spareribs, and fried won ton.

Battle of the South China Sea: An assortment of seafood in a rich sauce is plunged into a preparation of golden rice at your table. Enjoy the sound, aroma, and taste of this Cantonese specialty.

Millionaire's Chicken: A whole chicken is stuffed with black mushrooms, bamboo shoots, and pork and baked in its own clay mold, then cracked open just before serving. One day advance notice required.

Szechuan Gourmet Scallops or Prawns: Scallops served with a traditional western Chinese savory sauce in a unique flower basket. One day advance notice required.

Spicy Crisp Chicken: Boneless chicken, deep-fried until crisp, and coated with spicy Szechuan sauce; flavorful, tender, and moist.

MENU #1

China Pavilion Appetizers

O'Mei Vegetables (combination of four seasonal vegetables)

Chung King Prawns (prawns sautéed with garlic, ginger, and a hot Szechuan sauce)

Mongolian Beef

Chicken with Bean Sauce

Steamed Rice

MENU #2

Sizzling Rice Soup

Szechuan Gourmet Scallops or Prawns

Spicy Crisp Chicken

Barbecued Pork with Chinese Greens

Eggplant, Szechuan Style (stir-fried eggplant with a spicy sauce)

Steamed Rice

MENU #3

Millionaire's Chicken *or* Battle of the South China Sea

Fried Dumplings

Prawns with Lobster Sauce

Orange-flavored Beef

Chinese Greens with Oyster Sauce

Steamed Rice

CHINA STATION $$

700 University Avenue (near University Avenue off ramp)
Berkeley
Telephone: (415) 548-7880
Cusine: Cantonese

Hours:
    11:30 A.M.–1:00 A.M., daily

Credit cards: AE, MC, Visa
Full bar until 2:00 A.M.
Reservations recommended

China Station is one of the busiest and most impressive Chinese restaurants in the East Bay. Located near the University Avenue off ramp on Highway 80, the restaurant's reputation for outstanding food attracts natives from San Francisco's Chinatown, locals from all over the East Bay, and travelers who want a late supper.

The station, built in 1912, was a Southern Pacific depot, one of the last stops on the long journey west. The exterior's original Mission architecture has been skillfully maintained, and the interior has been redone in woods and brick that evoke the flavor of the building's era. The foot-thick exterior walls were filled with polyurethane to minimize the rumble of the passing trains, which chug by about every twenty minutes and can be viewed from window tables.

China Station, owned by third- and fourth-generation Chinese-Americans, is dedicated to the Chinese who helped build the transcontinental railroad. A collection of historical photographs showing these workers hangs on the walls of the main dining area.

The menu lists many dishes based on ones brought to this country by the first Chinese immigrants. Many of the preparations depend on seasonal availability of ingredients, so the menu changes with the seasons. If you do not like MSG added to your food, you can request that the kitchen not use it in the dishes you are served.

This spacious establishment is professionally run by owner-host Alon Yu, a member of the family that owns the Imperial Palace in San Francisco. Mr. Yu is often on hand to insure that your dining experience is a pleasant one.

Specialties

Dried Scallop Soup
Cantonese Chicken Salad
Five Willows Fillet of Rock Cod: Deep-fried fillet of rock cod with slivered
   bamboo shoots, mushrooms, yellow onions, green onions, and celery in
   a sweet and sour sauce.
Sautéed Clams in Garlic Sauce
Crab with Fresh Ginger and Scallions (seasonal)
Crab in Black Bean Sauce (seasonal)

MENU #1

Fried Pork Dumplings

Dried Scallop Soup

Broccoli in Oyster Sauce

Beef Steak Kau (steak cubes)

Black Mushroom Chicken

Sweet and Sour Pork *or* Five Willows Fillet of Rock Cod

Steamed Rice

MENU #2

Cantonese Chicken Salad

Sizzling Rice Soup

Sautéed Clams in Garlic Sauce

Straw Mushroom Chicken

Mongolian Lamb *or* Beef

Steamed Whole Rock Cod *or* Whole Rock Cod in Sweet and Sour Sauce

Steamed Rice

MENU #3

Scallops with Vegetables

Almond Chicken *or* Black Mushroom Chicken

Broccoli in Oyster Sauce

Barbecued Pork with Chinese Tender Greens

Kung Pao Prawns

Steamed Rice

COLONEL LEE'S MONGOLIAN BAR-BE-CUE $

3505 Clayton Road (near Bart station)
Concord
Telephone: (415) 798-1157
Cuisine: Mongolian

Hours:
    11:30 A.M.–9:00 P.M., Tuesday–Thursday
    11:30 A.M.–10:00 P.M., Friday and Saturday
    4:00 P.M.–9:00 P.M., Sunday

No credit cards
Beer and wine only

Look in the window of Colonel Lee's and you will see the chef cook a meal in seconds on a large cauldron-shaped grill. This simple, unique method of cooking, the Mongolian barbecue, has a dedicated following in the Bay Area. Mongolian cuisine derives from the campfire meals of the Mongolians, a nomadic people. Meats and vegetables are sliced into bite-sized pieces and quickly cooked on a huge, round griddle.

Upon entering Colonel Lee's, you are immediately served appetizers. After you have finished, a waitress guides you to the food stations where you take a bowl, select sliced, chilled meats and vegetables of your choice, and season them with the available sauces. There are four sauces: mild sweet, regular, spicy, and hot and spicy. You then give your bowl of uncooked food to the chef, who cooks it right before you. The griddle, heated to 900 degrees, cooks one serving in less than thirty seconds. When you return to your table, a bowl of hot steamed rice is waiting for you.

An egg roll, your bowl of selected foods, and steamed rice can be ordered for a mere $3.00. For a little bit more, two fried shrimps or two pieces of fried fish can be ordered with your bowl. Another luncheon choice is to select your combination of chilled meat and vegetables, have the chef cook it on the grill, then ask the waiter to take the barbecue back into the kitchen and place it on a warmed Mu Shu Pork wrapper, which is rolled up and garnished with plum sauce. Try this with hot, steamed rice. Delicious!

For dinner, the menu at Colonel Lee's includes "all you can eat" of soup, appetizers, the barbecue, rice, biscuits, cookies, and tea. Advantages of the Mongolian barbecue are obvious: patrons can choose the kinds and amounts of meat and vegetables, and the degree of spiciness by the choices of sauces.

At this immaculate, neighborhood eating spot you will always get a complete, satisfying meal for a very reasonable price.

ENCHANTED PAGODA $$

6516 Moraga Avenue (Montclair district)
Oakland
Telephone: (415) 339-2005
Cuisine: Mandarin

Hours:
   11:30 A.M.–11:00 P.M., Monday–Friday
   3:00 P.M.–11:00 P.M., Saturday and Sunday

Credit cards: MC, Visa
Full bar
Reservations recommended for six or more

A local resident of thirty years has opened the Enchanted Pagoda in Oakland's charming Montclair district. As you open the wooden doors and walk by the bar, a warm, inviting fire greets you on cold, wintry days. In the candle-lit modern interior, Montclairians often sip on such exotic drinks as "red dragon" and "blue Hawaii" while waiting for their dinners to be served.

Lou han jai, stir-fried broccoli, carrots, bamboo shoots, gingko nuts, straw mushrooms, and dried black mushrooms in a special sauce, is one of the most popular dishes here. Another house specialty is the Hong Kong chicken, tender fillets of chicken dipped in a special egg batter, fried crisp, and served over Chinese greens and baby mushrooms. If you like curry, try the sa cha beef, slices of beef cooked in a sa cha sauce flavored with curry.

The Enchanted Pagoda offers some outstanding food in a comfortable and relaxing atmosphere. You will be charmed by this place.

Specialties

Potstickers
Mandarin Hot and Sour Soup
Mu Shu Pork
Hong Kong Chicken: Boneless chicken dipped in special egg batter, fried crisp, and served with a variety of Chinese vegetables.
Lou Han Chai: Braised assorted vegetables—broccoli, carrots, bamboo shoots, gingko nuts, straw mushrooms—cooked in red bean curd sauce.
Crispy Kuo Teh: Fried potstickers.

MENU #1

Potstickers

Mandarin Hot and Sour Soup

Hong Kong Chicken

Lou Han Chai

Mongolian Beef

Steamed Rice

MENU #2

Sizzling Rice Soup

Chicken Chili Sauce

Mu Shu Pork

Mandarin Crab (seasonal) *or* Fish Slices with Sweet and Sour Sauce

Steamed Rice

MENU #3

Prawns with Cashew Nuts

Mandarin Duck

Black Mushrooms with Chicken

Beef with Vegetables *or* Asparagus with Steak Cubes (seasonal)

Steamed Rice

JADE PAGODA $$

1923 University Avenue (near Grove)
Berkeley
Telephone: (415) 843-1535
Cuisine: Cantonese and some Mandarin dishes

Hours:
    11:30 A.M.–10:00 P.M., Tuesday–Sunday

Credit cards: MC, Visa
Wine and beer only

This clean, cheerful-looking neighborhood restaurant caters to both local residents and business people. Opened in 1968, Jade Pagoda became so popular that it enlarged to twice its original size in 1975. The friendly chef and owner, Benny Wong, will greet you with a broad smile if you show even the slightest gesture of contentment over his creations.

The restaurant has a large luncheon menu, with Chinese and American plate lunches for reasonable prices. There is also a large number of dishes that can be ordered a la carte for lunch or dinner. One of our favorites is asparagus with beef in black bean sauce over rice or noodles.

Specialties

Chef's Special Sauce Chicken: Tender pieces of chicken stir-fried in a
    special sauce.
Chicken with Green Pepper and Black Bean Sauce (spicy)
Sang Chow Fried Rice Noodles: Stir-fried thin rice noodles with meat and
    mixed vegetables, with or without curry sauce.
Black Mushrooms in Oyster Sauce
Prawns with Chinese Greens

MENU #1

Lychee Chicken (pieces of chicken stir-fried with lychees in sweet and sour sauce)
Black Mushrooms in Oyster Sauce *or* Black Mushrooms with Greens
Almond Pressed Duck
Snow Peas with Beef
Steamed Rice

MENU #2

Chef's Special Sauce Chicken
Parchment-wrapped Beef
Sliced Fish with Straw Mushrooms
Prawns with Curry Sauce *or* Prawns with Black Bean Sauce
Steamed Rice

MENU #3

Mushrooms and Pork Soup
Prawns with Chinese Greens
Beef with Oyster Sauce
Chicken with Double Mushrooms
Steamed Rice

JASMINE $$

14272 San Pablo Avenue (near El Portal Shopping Center)
San Pablo
Telephone: (415) 235-6845
Cuisine: Cantonese

Hours:

    11:30 A.M.–9:00 P.M., Tuesday–Thursday

    11:30 A.M.–10:30 P.M., Friday

    4:00 P.M.–10:30 P.M., Saturday

    12:30 P.M.–9:00 P.M., Sunday

Credit Cards: MC, Visa

Full bar

Reservations needed for five or more

Free parking lot

    Because of the great demand for good Chinese food in the San Pablo area, owner Ray Foo enlarged his Jasmine restaurant, expanding not only the dining area, but also adding a bar and banquet facilities. The restaurant is filled during the early afternoon hours with business people who usually order the combination luncheon plates. These plates include soup of the day, the entree over rice or noodles, and dessert.

    During the dinner hours, the locals from Richmond, San Pablo, and Pinole come to enjoy the good food, comfortable, air-conditioned atmosphere, and exceptional service, all of which Mr. Foo considers essential for his customers. For example, as each dish is served, the waiter announces what it is and then serves each diner individually.

    If you would like some help in planning your meal, the waiters or Mr. Foo will be glad to assist you.

Specialties

Stuffed Chicken Wings: Boned chicken wings, stuffed with chicken meat, mushrooms, green onions, and pork, then deep-fried and served with a special sauce.

Butterfly Prawns

Wor Bar Sup Gum: Deep-fried rice patty with nine colorful and tasty ingredients that sizzles when it is served; not listed on the menu.

Mongolian Beef

Jasmine Imperial Prawns: Deep-fried prawns served in a delicate sauce.

Lunch Menu Recommendations

Fried Prawns

Barbecued Spareribs

Parchment-wrapped Beef

Tomato Beef Chow Mein
Jasmine Chicken Chow Mein
Jasmine Special Yee Won Ton

MENU #1

Butterfly Prawns

Diced Winter Melon Soup

Beef with Chinese Long Beans (seasonal) *or* Mongolian Beef

Lemon Chicken

Wor Bar Sup Gum

Steamed Rice

MENU #2

Sizzling Rice Soup

Pressed Mandarin Duck

Szechuan Prawns

Chinese Greens Sauté

Jasmine Imperial Prawns

Steamed Rice

MENU #3

Stuffed Chicken Wings

Beef over Snow

Chicken with Snow Peas

Yang Chow Fried Rice

Crab in Black Bean Sauce (seasonal) *or* Shrimp with Lobster Sauce

KING TSIN $$

1699 Solano Avenue (near Tulare)
Berkeley
Telephone: (415) 525-9890
Cuisine: Mandarin

Hours:
11:30 A.M.–2:00 P.M., 4:30 P.M.–9:30 P.M., Wednesday–Monday

Credit cards: MC, Visa

A favorite neighborhood restaurant in the north Berkeley area, King Tsin opened in 1967. Within five years the long lines demanded an expansion to more than double the capacity. The facade created in the remodeling makes it impossible to miss King Tsin. The horizontally shaped brick building, with red columns and doors and a green tile roof, stands out distinctively from the surrounding buildings as you drive up Solano Avenue.

The food here is always reliable. Some favorites include potstickers and sweet and sour whole fish. Be sure to try the Mandarin glazed apples or bananas for dessert. The fruit is dipped in batter, deep-fried, coated in a sugar mixture, and immersed in ice-cold water. This exquisite dessert is crunchy on the outside and smooth on the inside.

Specialties

Potstickers
Mu Shu Pork
Mandarin Glazed Bananas or Apples
Hot and Sour Soup
Sizzling Rice Soup
Sweet and Sour Whole Fish

MENU #1

Potstickers

Sizzling Rice Soup

Sweet and Sour Whole Fish

Spiced Shrimp

Bean Curd with Ground Pork

Steamed Rice

MENU #2

Hot and Sour Soup

Crispy Spiced Duck with Steamed Buns (order a half duck)

Mandarin Meatballs with Chinese Greens

Ming's Beef (stir-fried beef with mixed vegetables)

Steamed Rice

MENU #3

Cold Spiced Beef with Cucumber

Sizzling Rice Shrimp

Northern-style Vegetables Covered with Eggs

Chef's Special (scallops stir-fried with fish and chicken slices and braised in wine
   sauce)

Crab in Black Bean and Ginger Sauce (seasonal) *or* Steamed Whole Fish

Steamed Rice

KING TU $$

1335 Solano Avenue
Albany
Telephone: (415) 525-2285
Cuisine: Mandarin and Szechuan

Hours:
   11:00 A.M.–9:45 P.M., Monday, Tuesday, and Thursday
   11:00 A.M.–10:30 P.M., Friday and Saturday
   4:00 P.M.–9:45 P.M., Sunday

Credit cards: BC, MC
Full bar
Reservations needed for four or more

   King Tu is the only Chinese restaurant in Berkeley that specializes in
both Mandarin cuisine and the spicier Szechuan. Owner Yu-Chia Yao
owned a restaurant in Korea for many years, speaks fluent Korean, and
will often prepare the Mandarin dishes with a Szechuan flair for those
Koreans who venture here from as far away as Concord, San Jose, and
Sacramento.

This is a family-run, neighborhood restaurant. The tall, young, pretty hostess, Jenny Yao, is a niece of the owner. You can convey your preferences on how spicy you want your food to her, the waiter, or the cook himself.

Specialties

Potstickers
Sautéed Snow Peas
Hot Braised Fish: Whole, fresh rock cod prepared with finely chopped water chestnuts, mushrooms, bamboo shoots, hot pepper, and special bean sauce.
Szechuan Chicken: Chicken stir-fried in a spicy sauce.
Clay-baked Chicken: A fowl that is finely flavored, stuffed with mushrooms and bamboo shoots, then encased in clay and baked.

MENU #1

Potstickers
Hot and Sour Soup
Mu Shu Pork
Hot Braised Fish
Sautéed Snow Peas (seasonal)
Steamed Rice

MENU #2

Sizzling Rice Soup
Mu Shu Pork
Princess Chicken (tender pieces of chicken sautéed in hot bean sauce)
Crab in Black Bean Sauce (seasonal) *or* Prawns in Black Bean Sauce
Szechuan Beef
Steamed Rice

MENU #3

Sizzling Rice Shrimp
Sautéed Abalone, Scallop, and Chicken Meat

Szechuan Meatballs with Vegetables

Hot Bean Curd (spicy bean cake with minced pork)

Snow White Chicken (tender pieces of chicken, delicately cooked with mushrooms and snow peas in egg white sauce)

Steamed Rice

THE LANTERN $$

814 Webster Street (near 9th)
Oakland
Telephone: (415) 451-0627
Cuisine: Cantonese

Hours:
    11:00 A.M.–11:00 P.M., daily

Credit cards: AE, BC, MC
Full bar
Free parking

The Lantern is the oldest restaurant in Oakland's Chinatown and the only one in the area with its own parking lot.

The Chor Wongs opened the restaurant in 1947, with Mr. and Mrs. Wong acting as the cooks. Since then, the Lantern has expanded twice to accommodate its growing clientele. The restaurant is very modern, intimate, and tastefully decorated with Oriental decor. As you enter, a large bar is on the left and the dining area is on the right, extending inward in a T shape. Wood dominates the interior design—wooden beams and wooden panels accented with bamboo—and gold wallpaper with Chinese murals covers the walls. The setting makes you feel as if you are in an Oriental inn.

Son Dick Wong trains the uniformed waiters and is insistent that they extend good service to the customers. This clean, cozy restaurant is a favorite with many Oakland old-timers and the nearby business community. The energetic senior owners, who often greet guests and oversee the dining room so that there are no disgruntled patrons, lend much charm to the experience of dining here.

Specialties

Soy Sauce Chicken (served on Sunday only)
Stir-fried Scallops
Deep-fried Scallops
Crispy Chicken
Mongolian Beef
Chicken with Red Chili Pepper: Chicken fillets, red chili pepper, and green bell pepper stir-fried in hoisin sauce.
Sweet and Sour Pork Chops: Deep-fried pork chops served with sweet and sour sauce; not listed on the menu.

Lunch Menu Recommendations

Tomato Beef Chow Mein
Gold and Silver Chow Mein: Two types of noodles, wheat and rice, stir-fried together.
Duck Yee Foo Won Ton: Deep-fried won tons with duck and vegetables in gravy.
Crispy Chicken
Barbecued Spareribs

MENU #1

Egg Flower Soup *or* Won Ton Soup

Combination Special (fried prawns, foil-wrapped chicken, fried won ton, and barbecued pork)

Clams in Black Bean Sauce

Abalone with Black Mushrooms

Steamed Whole Rock Cod

Steamed Rice

MENU #2

Abalone Soup *or* Dried Scallops Soup

Stir-fried Scallops with Vegetables

Cantonese Chicken Salad

Mongolian Beef *or* Beef with Asparagus (seasonal)

Pressed Mandarin Duck

Oyster Sauce Gai Lan (Chinese broccoli) *or* Sweet and Sour Pork Chops

Steamed Rice

MENU #3

Crispy Chicken *or* Soy Sauce Chicken

Crab with Egg Sauce (seasonal) *or* Crab in Black Bean Sauce (seasonal) *or*
   Chicken in Black Bean Sauce

Barbecued Pork with Snow Peas

Beef Steak Kau (stir-fried steak, Chinese style)

Black Mushrooms in Oyster Sauce

Steamed Rice

MANDARIN GARDENS $$

2025 Shattuck Avenue (near University)
Berkeley
Telephone: (415) 848-4849
Cuisine: Mandarin

Hours:
   11:30 A.M.–2:30 P.M., 4:30 P.M.–9:30 P.M., daily

Credit cards: BA, Visa

   The City of Berkeley is fortunate that one of the most accomplished chefs from the Orient decided to open a restaurant there. Northern-China-born Tak Hang Wong was a supervisor of chefs in two large hotels in the Orient for many years before becoming a Berkeley restaurateur.

   Chef Tak does a superb job of blending complementary flavors and contrasting textures. For example, mashed chicken soup consists of chunks of chicken, slices of abalone, shrimp, and peas mixed in a light, creamy white base. The toast shrimp are dipped in a sweet and sour sauce and rolled in a special dry pepper mixture. There is also a reasonably priced lunch menu for the business crowd.

Mandarin Gardens' interior is tastefully done in a woods theme, with a miniature grotto and engraved glass. The restaurant is family operated, with Tak's daughter and son assisting as hostess and waiter. His son-in-law, Ming Choi Cheung, has a great repertoire of wok dishes. This place is tops on our list for its superb food, pleasant surroundings, and friendly service.

Specialties

Chinese Fire Pot: Assorted meats, fish, shellfish, and Chinese vegetables cooked at the table by the diners; during the winter season only.
Crab in Black Bean Sauce (seasonal)
Spiced Prawns
"Snow Flower" Shrimp Balls: Minced shrimp meat coated with a light batter, and deep-fried.
Whole Fish with Sweet and Sour Sauce: Boneless deep-fried fish, served with sweet and sour sauce.
Mu Shu Pork

MENU #1

Hot and Sour Soup

Spiced Prawns

"Snow Flower" Shrimp Balls

Sliced Fish with Wine Sauce

Mu Shu Pork

Steamed Rice

MENU #2

Potstickers

Sizzling Rice Soup

Beef with Snow Peas

Whole Fish with Sweet and Sour Sauce

Straw Mushrooms with Green Vegetables

Steamed Rice

MENU #3

Sliced Chicken with Egg White Sauce

Crab in Black Bean Sauce (seasonal) *or* Mu Shu Pork

Mandarin Meatballs with Vegetables (spicy)

Bean Curd with Minced Meat (spicy bean cake with minced pork)

Shredded Beef with Green Pepper

Steamed Rice

MANDARIN VILLAGE $$

3594 Mt. Diablo Boulevard
Lafayette
Telephone: (415) 283-2141
Cuisine: Mandarin

Hours:
    4:30 P.M.–9:15 P.M., daily

Credit cards: MC, Visa

The bamboo-patterned wallpaper, gold tablecloths, gold carpeting, red napkins, and red candle on each table here create the perfect atmosphere for intimate dining, a setting reminiscent of small restaurants along the Seine. But once the food arrives, it is very definitely Chinese!

The potstickers are delicious, and the sizzling rice soup sizzles loudly when the rice crusts touch the delicate broth filled with shrimp, bamboo shoots, peas, and other delights. The exquisite princess chicken is one of the highlights of this place, and the combination of ingredients in vegetables deluxe blends beautifully—smooth, rough, crunchy, and soft. The hot peppers in General Tsuo's chicken should stimulate your palate to try even more of the fine dishes at Mandarin Village. You will be pleasantly surprised at the moderate prices charged for such exceptional atmosphere and food.

Specialties

Potstickers

Princess Chicken: Boneless chicken balls marinated in delicate spices, dipped in water chestnut flour, deep-fried, then stir-fried with mushrooms, peas, and carrots.

General Tsuo's Chicken: Diced chicken stir-fried in a spicy sauce.

Happy Family: A delicious combination of abalone, shrimp, sliced breast of chicken, pork, quail eggs, and vegetables.

Vegetables Deluxe

MENU #1

Potstickers

Sizzling Rice Soup

General Tsuo's Chicken

Mongolian Barbecued Beef

Hot Bean Sauce Braised Fish (seasonal) *or* Hot Sauce Shrimp (shrimp are deep-fried, then cooked in a Szechuan sauce)

Steamed Rice

MENU #2

Hot and Sour Soup

Princess Chicken

Mu Shu Pork

Vegetables Deluxe

Happy Family

Steamed Rice

MENU #3

Hot Spiced Chicken

Smoked Tea Duck (order a half duck)

Manchurian Beef (slices of beef stir-fried in a spice and wine sauce)

Seafood Supreme (combination of abalone, shrimp, and sliced chicken breast in a wine sauce)

Steamed Rice

ON LUCK $$

387 9th Street
Oakland
Telephone: (415) 834-5141
Cuisine: Cantonese
Hours:
    11:00 A.M.–9:00 P.M., Wednesday–Monday

No credit cards

This is surely one of the best family-style restaurants in Oakland, popular with both the local Chinese and people who work in the Civic Center area. Lee On, owner and chef, was formerly a cook at another popular restaurant in Oakland, and before that, a cook for many years in Hong Kong. The fine food served here is achieved by using quality ingredients and no shortcuts in preparation. And unlike many Chinese restaurants, MSG is used very sparingly.

Hard-working, diligent On takes great pride and care in preparing each dish individually and is concerned that his food is pleasing to his customers. For example, in some restaurants the chow fun noodles are starchy and stick together. At On Luck each sheet of fun is cut separately, so that when the noodles are stir-fried, they brown evenly and the seasonings are distributed throughout. To test the culinary achievements of the chef, try such dishes as chicken stuffed with sweet rice or Peking duck.

Lee On will often come out to greet and talk with his customers. The stately, smiling woman who may collect your check or open the door for you as you depart is Mrs. Lee. She makes sure that the service is meticulous.

Specialties

Butterfly Prawns
Chicken with Sweet Rice Stuffing (one day advance notice)
Chicken with Ginger Oil Sauce: Mild-flavored ginger oil sauce is poured
    over bite-sized pieces of chicken; one of the best in town.
Peking Duck (one day advance notice)
Steak Cubes with Tender Greens
Beef and Bok Choy Chow Fun
Clams with Black Bean Sauce

MENU #1

Bean Cakes in Pork Soup

Butterfly Prawns

Chinese Broccoli with Chicken

Abalone with Oyster Sauce

Sweet Peas with Shrimp

Steamed Rice

MENU #2

Cantonese Fried Chicken Wings

Shrimp with Lobster Sauce

Beef with Oyster Sauce

Pressed Duck

Sautéed Chinese Greens

Yang Chow Fried Rice

MENU #3

Clams with Black Bean Sauce

Steamed Rock Cod

Steak Cubes with Tender Greens

Chow Ming Young (fine-cut Sirloin of beef, cooked with mixed vegetables, and crowned with crisp rice-stick noodles)

Cashew Nut Prawns

Steamed Rice

ON ON $

702 Webster Street (near 7th)
Oakland
Telephone: (415) 452-0568
Cuisine: Cantonese

Hours:
    8:00 A.M.–6:00 P.M., Wednesday–Monday

No credit cards

    Early in the morning this small restaurant is bustling with Chinese eating bowls of congee, thick rice soup containing various kinds of meat, poultry, or seafood. A deep-fried puff is sliced and eaten with it.
    This restaurant is also known for its noodle and won ton dishes. In the early morning hours (before the congee crowd arrives), won ton skins and vermicelli-thin noodles are prepared in the kitchen. As a result, the noodles served here are lighter, thinner, and tastier than in many restaurants.
    On On is great for a quick lunch or snack, and the waiters are very attentive and courteous. Many people from downtown Oakland walk to On On to lunch on the noodle and won ton dishes. The rice-plate lunches are also a good choice and you'll be surprised how satisfying they can be. They'll keep you filled all day.

Specialties

Won Ton Soup: This is not the usual won ton soup. The filling has a great
    deal of shrimp, and the broth is especially good.
Won Ton Noodle Soup
Rib of Beef: Chinese-style beef stew with Oriental seasonings. Order it
    with won ton soup or won ton noodle soup.
On On Special Chow Mein: Shrimp, chicken, mushrooms, barbecued
    pork, pork tripe, and Chinese greens mixed with noodles. May be
    ordered without the pork tripe, if desired.
On On Special Chow Fun: Same as above, but with rice noodles.
Hong-Kong-style Beef Chow Mein *or* Pork Chow Mein: Beef or pork with
    mushrooms and bean sprouts, served over crispy pan-fried noodles.
Tender Greens in Oyster Sauce: Excellent accompaniment to any of the
    above dishes.

Congee Recommendations

Combination Congee
Beef Congee
Shrimp Congee

Fresh Julienne Chicken Congee
Meatball Congee
"Deep-fried Puff": Chinese deep-fried cruller; excellent with any of the
   congees.

Chow Mein or Chow Fun Recommendations

On On Special Chow Fun
Beef and Tender Greens Chow Fun
Combination Chow Fun: Chicken, barbecued pork, and abalone.
On On Special Chow Mein
Julienne Chicken Chow Mein
Shrimp and Tender Greens Chow Mein
Hong-Kong-style Beef *or* Pork Chow Mein

Rice Plate Recommendations

Curry Beef *or* Chicken with Rice
Beef and Tender Greens with Rice
Mushroom and Chicken in Oyster Sauce with Rice
Shrimp *or* Beef and Egg with Rice: The egg in this dish is not "scrambled,"
   but instead has a very smooth texture and a delicious flavor.
Spareribs in Black Bean Sauce with Rice
Beef and Tomato with Rice
Shrimp and Tender Greens with Rice

POINT ORIENT $$

199 Park Place
Point Richmond
Telephone: (415) 237-4999
Cuisine: Mandarin

Hours:
   11:30 A.M.–10:00 P.M., Tuesday–Wednesday
   11:30 A.M.–11:00 P.M., Friday and Saturday
   4:00 P.M.–10:00 P.M., Sunday

Credit cards: BA, MC
Full bar
Reservations needed for five or more
Free parking lot

Majestic Victorian houses perch on the hillside, with sweeping views of the meeting points of three bay bridges, private coves, and beaches. This is Point Richmond, considered by many old-timers to be a town quite separate from downtown Richmond. Point Orient is situated opposite the town plaza, and close by are quaint shops, old saloons, and coffee houses.

The building the restaurant occupies was the first movie theater in the East Bay. It opened on Februrary 15, 1913, to a capacity crowd of 1,200, and was a success until television became popular during the early 1960s. The ceiling and brick walls of the original building remain, but the interior has been completely remodeled to create a comfortable and spacious area for dining.

The owners Dave Lee and Bob Young have successfully maintained high quality food preparation and good service over the years.

Banquets prepared in any one of the six major Chinese cuisines may be arranged ahead of time at Point Orient.

Specialties

Imperial Prawns: Deep-fried prawns served in a delicate sauce.
Point Orient Soufflé: Abalone, ham, and egg white in a delicate cream
  sauce.
Point Orient Iron Chicken: Pieces of boneless chicken dipped in a light
  batter, deep-fried, served with a delicate sauce, and garnished with
  chopped green onions.
Parchment Beef
Shredded Chicken, Barbecued Pork, and Abalone with Vegetables

Menu #1

Mushroom and Egg Flower Soup

Point Orient Soufflé

Beef with Snow Peas *or* Beef with Black Mushrooms

Shredded Chicken, Barbecued Pork, and Abalone with Vegetables

Steamed Rice

MENU #2

Parchment Beef

Szechuan Prawns

Crab Meat with Fluffed Eggs

Snow Peas with Black Mushrooms

Yang Chow Fried Rice

MENU #3

Point Orient Iron Chicken

Almond Chicken Ding

Abalone with Oyster Sauce

Prawns Imperial

Steamed Rice

SILVER DRAGON $$

835 Webster Street (near 9th)
Oakland
Telephone: (415) 893-3748
Cuisine: Cantonese

Hours:
    11:30 A.M.–10:00 P.M., daily

Credit cards: MC, Visa
Full bar

You will enjoy dining in the contemporary, spacious, informal atmosphere of the Silver Dragon, one of Oakland's oldest and largest eating establishments. The owners, the Chee family, have two chefs. The head chef, a member of the Chee family with two generations of cooking experience behind him, has extensive knowledge of what people want in good dining. Besides the traditional dishes on the menu, there is the very popular "every day" menu. Ask what fresh fish, seafood, and vegetables are available and they will be prepared for you in a variety of interesting ways. For example, seasonal fish are steamed or fried with a number of different sauces.

The second chef is from Hong Kong and specializes in the banquet menu. Many local Chinese come to eat classic banquet dishes on special occasions, such as Chinese New Year, birthdays, or other holidays. One of these dishes is stuffed cocktail crab claws. The claws are halved, stuffed with crab meat, fish cake, and other ingredients, and then deep-fried to a golden brown. An exotic fish cake from Hawaii is brought in by air for the snow flower fish balls.

A full bar is available on both floors of this family-style, family-run, no-frills-service restaurant. Because the Silver Dragon is popular for banquets, call in advance for dinner reservations, especially on weekends. Manager Lester Chee suggests the "every day menu" specials as the most economical, if the selections suit you.

Specialties

Deep-fried Shrimp Balls (not listed on the menu)
Pressed Mandarin Duck
Steak Cubes Cantonese
Five Fragrance Spiced Pork, Szechuan: Finely sliced pork, onion, green
    pepper, and spicy turnips.
Crispy Chicken
Dragon Cod Cantonese: Deep-fried sweet and sour rock cod.

MENU #1

Pineapple Chicken

Shrimp with Chinese Greens

Beef with Asparagus (seasonal) *or* Steak Cubes Cantonese

Five Fragrance Spiced Pork, Szechuan

Steamed Rice

MENU #2

Diced Winter Melon Soup

Parchment Chicken

Four Seasons Beef, Shanghai Style (beef slices sautéed with bamboo shoots, water
    chestnuts, mushrooms, and vegetables)

Mandarin Pressed Duck

Deep-fried Shrimp Balls

Steamed Rice

MENU #3

Hong Tao Yee Won Ton

Oyster Sauce Abalone

Steamed Rock Cod

Curry Chicken *or* Chicken Salad

Deep-fried Oysters

Steamed Rice

SZECHUAN VILLAGE $$

548 West Contra Costa Boulevard
Pleasant Hill
Telephone: (415) 671-0655
Cuisine: Szechuan

Hours:
  11:30 A.M.–10:00 P.M., daily

Credit cards: MC, Visa
Full bar
Reservations advised
Parking available

"Good evening, Mr. Jones. How are you today?" says Mr. Richard Chin, as he extends his hand to greet his customer. Then he leads Mr. Jones and his guest to a quiet corner table in one of the three semidivided rooms of the restaurant. Greeting most of his customers by name seems to be a common practice of the personable Chin, one of the three brothers who own the restaurant. He says that 90 percent of his customers return, and they become his friends.

The restaurant is tastefully done both inside and out in various woods. An enchanting garden with pond, hand-carved wooden room dividers, and delicate bamboo branches etched on glass windows give the place a unified, serene, earthy atmosphere, and the earthenware place settings on inlaid wooden tables add to the overall look.

Minimal gestures will bring instant recognition from the passing waiters, and the style of service here surpasses that usually encountered in

Chinese family-style restaurants. For example, when you have finished your appetizers, the plates are removed and you are given fresh dinner plates.

Across San Francisco Bay in Daly City, there is a second Szechuan Village (page 146).

Specialties

Potstickers
Sizzling Rice Soup
Mu Shu Pork
Lamb à la Hunan: Sliced leg of lamb sautéed with leeks, bamboo shoots, and hot pepper sauce.

MENU #1

Potstickers

Sizzling Rice Soup

Braised Eggplant with Garlic Sauce

Lamb à la Hunan

Smoked Tea Duck with Steamed Buns (order a half duck)

Steamed Rice

MENU #2

Hot and Sour Soup

Szechuan Fried Spareribs

Mongolian Beef

Mu Shu Pork

Steamed Rice

MENU #3

Snow Peas with Black Mushrooms and Water Chestnuts

Diced Chicken, Szechuan Style (spicy)

Spicy Ma Po Bean Curd

Sizzling Rice Shrimp

Snow Peas with Beef

Steamed Rice

TAIWAN RESTAURANT $$

2701 University Avenue (near Shattuck)
Berkeley
Telephone: (415) 845-1456
Cuisine: Mandarin and Taiwanese

Hours:
   11:30 A.M.–9:30 P.M., Monday–Friday
   10:30 A.M.–9:30 P.M., Saturday and Sunday

Credit cards: AE, BA, MC, Visa
Wine and beer only
Reservations needed for four or more

Taiwan, the largest island off the coast of Mainland China, has long been a refuge for people leaving all areas of that country. Among the immigrants have been master chefs, who brought with them their culinary skills and regional dishes. In Taiwan, these dishes were further influenced by the island's native cuisine. Taiwan Restaurant manager William Sang says that his place and Shang Yuen in San Francisco are the only restaurants in the United States that serve Taiwanese-style Chinese cuisine. Both are owned by Lin Shui Ho, a former resident of Taiwan.

The menu is quite diverse, with specialties from Manuchuria, Peking, Shangtung, Shanghai, Hunan, and Canton, as well as Taiwan. A delicious lunch, which includes soup, entrée, fruit, and tea, is served for a very reasonable price. Often times, two or three people can be seen feasting on a whole fish, an order of stir-fried vegetables, and steamed rice. A Chinese tea lunch, with such items as spring rolls and onion pancakes, is available on weekends.

The friendly, efficient staff will make your visit to the Taiwan a very enjoyable one.

Specialties

General Tsuo's Chicken: Cubes of chicken prepared with a hot and sour
   wine sauce.
Smoked Tea Duck
Mongolian Beef *or* Lamb
Yang Chow Lion's Head: Pork balls deep-fried, then braised in brown
   bean sauce with Chinese cabbage.

Lunch Menu (weekends only)

Chinese doughnuts
Fried Biscuits
Green Onion Cake
Pork Noodle Soup
Beef Noodle Soup
Fish Balls in Clear Broth with Chopped Green Onions

MENU #1

Hot and Sour Soup

Spicy Braised Fish

Smoked Tea Duck (order a half duck)

Asparagus Beef (seasonal) *or* Snow Peas with Beef

Spiced Prawns

Steamed Rice

MENU #2

Sizzling Rice Soup

General Tsuo's Chicken

Braised Green Beans

Mu Shu Pork

Potstickers

MENU #3

Fisherman's Soup (shrimp, scallops, and abalone)

Shrimp with Snow Peas

Crispy Chicken (order a half chicken)

Sautéed Bok Choy Hearts

Velvet Chicken

Steamed Rice

YET WAH $$

4635 Clayton Road (one block from Treat)
Concord
Telephone: (415) 671-7044
Cuisine: Mandarin

Hours:
    11:30 A.M.–11:00 P.M., daily

Credit cards: AE, DC, MC, Visa
Full bar
Reservations needed for six or more

    You won't miss the Concord Yet Wah. The white, Chinese-design building, with its sweeping tile roof, stands out distinctively. The two-storied interior is equally complete in its Oriental look. As you enter, the main wall displays a twenty-foot, nine-dragon panel of carved teak with gold leaf.

    The menu and specialties are similar to those at the San Francisco Yet Wah branches (page 82).

MARIN COUNTY

ASIA PALACE $$

Sir Francis Drake Boulevard and Olema Road
Fairfax
Telephone: (415) 456-3870
Cuisine: Mandarin

Hours:
    5:00 P.M–10:00 P.M., Sunday–Thursday
    5:00 P.M–10:30 P.M., Friday and Saturday

Credit cards: MC, Visa
Wine and beer only
Reservations recommended on weekends

Patrons from northern Marin County kept asking the owner of Asia Palace in San Rafael to open a restaurant closer to them. In 1979, this very attractive place, serving good Mandarin food, opened in Fairfax.

Park your car in front and walk by the patio to the entryway, where there is a creek that is lighted at night. Inside, a glowing fire greets guests on cold, wintry nights, and there are window seats that look out onto the creek. Booths line one side of the room and large round tables are in the center. Dim lights and pleasant music create the atmosphere for intimate dining. All of the decor, including white Chinese lanterns and Oriental art, is well coordinated to create a subtle, quiet elegance, making Asia Palace the kind of restaurant where you would bring a special person to celebrate an occasion.

Mr. Nieh and his son, Henry, manage the restaurant. The service is excellent and the food is delicious. The suggested menus and specialties are similar to those at the San Rafael branch.

ASIA PALACE $$

885–887 Fourth Street
San Rafael
Telephone: (415) 457-9977
Cuisine: Mandarin

Hours:
   11:00 A.M.–2:30 P.M., 5:00 P.M.–10:00 P.M., Monday, Wednesday and
      Thursday; until 11:00 P.M., Friday and Saturday
   11:00 A.M.–11:00 P.M., Sunday

Credit cards: MC, Visa

Since its opening in April 1976, Asia Palace has enjoyed steady patronage. Located downtown, it is a favorite lunch spot with the business community. During the dinner hours, patrons come from all areas of Marin County to dine on the fine food served here.

Most of the selections on the menu are properly prepared and delicious. For example, the egg rolls, a favorite here, have very thin skins encasing generous amounts of meat and vegetable filling. Though it is very difficult to wrap such a thin skin, Asia Palace does it perfectly each time.

This restaurant is run by Mrs. Nieh and her son. Patrons who had to drive from northern Marin County to dine here pestered them to open another branch. As a result, an Asia Palace has opened in Fairfax (page 120), and Marin County residents can now enjoy the same fine food at two locations.

Specialties

Potstickers
Mu Shu Pork
Chinese Barbecue Sauce Beef: Beef stir-fried in a spicy sauce.
Mongolian Beef
House Special Chicken with Vegetables: Chicken chunks with mixed vegetables stir-fried in a Szechuan spicy sauce.

MENU #1

Potstickers

Mongolian Beef

Mu Shu Pork

Shrimp with Cashew Nuts

Vegetable Combination

Steamed Rice

MENU #2

Mushrooms, Snow Peas, and Bamboo Shoots

Chinese Barbecue Sauce Beef

Spring Rolls (four)

Mu Shu Chicken

Hot Braised Whole Fish (order one day in advance)

Steamed Rice

Menu #3

Hot and Sour Soup

Broccoli Beef

Bamboo Shoots and Mushrooms with Pork

Scallops in Hot Spicy Sauce

House Special Chicken with Vegetables

Steamed Rice

NEW PEKING LOW RESTAURANT $$

411 Third Street (in the Montecito Shopping Center)
San Rafael
Telephone: (415) 456-9416
Cuisine: Mandarin and Szechuan

Hours:
11:30 A.M.–2:00 P.M., 4:30 P.M.–9:30 P.M., Monday–Thursday; until
10:00 P.M., Friday
noon–10:00 P.M., Saturday
4:30 P.M.–9:30 P.M., Sunday

Credit cards: MC, Visa
Wine and beer only
Reservations recommended on weekends

From the outside, the New Peking Low Restaurant looks quite small. Once inside, it is spacious and comfortable, with three rooms extending back into the building. The softly lit interior has Oriental lanterns, white linen cloths, and red napkins.

Friendly waiters will be glad to assist you with the ordering. The champagne fish, assorted soup in earthen pots, and Shangtung twin dish are just a few of the unique dishes at this fine restaurant. Stir-fried crab is offered when in season, and such favorites as deep-fried shrimp balls, spicy whole fish, chicken salad, and Peking duck can be ordered one day in advance for banquets or special-occasion dinners. From Monday through Friday, a reasonably priced, delicious luncheon plate is available. Beware: All of the dishes printed in red on the menu are hot and spicy.

Mr. Chang, chef and owner, has more than thirty years of experience in preparing Pekinese food. Residents of Marin County are fortunate to have him preparing genuine Mandarin cuisine.

Specialties

Shrimp Balls: Minced shrimp formed into balls, dipped into a light batter, and deep-fried.
Cold Plate: Cold cooked chicken, prawns, jellyfish, cucumber, and beef.
Peking Duck (order one day in advance)
Crab in Black Bean Sauce (seasonal)
Braised Fish with Brown Bean Sauce (order two hours in advance)
Assorted Soup in Earthen Pot: Prawns, chicken, sea cucumber, baby corn, bamboo shoots, and mushrooms.

MENU #1

Potstickers

Assorted Soups in Earthen Pot

Shangtung Twin Dish (one side of the dish has shredded pork in Peking bean sauce, the other side has stir-fried shredded chicken)

Mongolian Beef

Braised Fish with Brown Bean Sauce

Steamed Rice

MENU #2

Sizzling Rice Soup with Mixed Seafood

Mu Shu Pork

Chicken Fillet with Black Bean Sauce

Snow Peas, Water Chestnuts, and Mushrooms *or* Crab in Black Bean Sauce (seasonal)

Shrimp Balls

Steamed Rice

MENU #3

Mandarin Pork (seasoned, sliced pork coated with flour and egg, then stir-fried in Mandarin sauce)

Beef with Chinese Mushrooms and Bamboo Shoots

Steamed Fish with Black Beans

Cold Plate *or* Fried Prawns with Hot Pepper

Peking Vegetables Deluxe

Steamed Rice

YET WAH $$

2019 Larkspur Landing
Larkspur
Telephone: (415) 461-3631
Cuisine: Mandarin

Hours:
    11:30 A.M.–3:00 P.M., 4:00 P.M.–11:00 P.M., Monday–Saturday
    noon–10:00 P.M., Sunday

Credit cards: AE, DC, MC, Visa
Full bar
Reservations needed for six or more

This Yet Wah, with a panoramic view of the bay, is situated on three levels. As you enter, the bar and lounge are straight ahead, a very attractive and cozy area with glass doors opening onto a deck overlooking the bay. During the summer, cocktails and lunch can be taken on the deck. To the left of the entrance is the main dining room, which also has a nice view of the bay, and two steps up from the entrance is a second dining room.

A very reasonably priced "merchants lunch" is served here, with the entrées changing daily. The menu and specialties are similar to those at the San Francisco Yet Wah branches (page 82).

NAPA COUNTY

Located at the north end of the bay is the beautiful Napa Valley, an easy one-day motor trip from San Francisco. While in the valley, you may visit some of the many wineries, view the magnificent rural beauty of California, or perhaps watch golf stars compete in the annual Silverado Golf Tournament.

For those planning a trip to this area, there are three Chinese restaurants worth visiting. They are all family owned and headed by disciples of renowned chef, Wong Ngai Gong. Each establishment bears some similarity to the other, yet each is different in its own way. The diner will find that all three serve well-prepared meals at very reasonable prices.

Our Chinese friends will be happy to know that any of the above restaurants will accommodate your request for a traditional, family-style Chinese meal. Merely tell the owner the price you wish to spend and let him plan the menu. You will be relying on "pot luck" and the chef's imagination. We have often been pleasantly surprised by such a meal after a beautiful day in the Napa Valley.

CHINA CAFE $$

2940 Jefferson Street (near Pueblo)
Napa
Telephone: (707) 224-9320
Cuisine: Cantonese and American

Hours:
    3:30 P.M.–9:30 P.M., Wednesday–Monday

Credit cards: MC, Visa
Wine and beer only
Free parking lot

The interior of this restaurant is unique. The high cathedral ceiling and wood-paneled walls remind us of dining in an Oriental country inn and a warm, cozy atmosphere prevails throughout.

After being in business for many years in two different locations, David Shui and his family decided to open a restaurant specifically designed to reflect their tastes. The result, built in 1977, is a joy to visit, both esthetically and gastronomically. All of Mr. Shui's five children started assisting in the restaurant's operation when they were four or five years old. Even though most of the children are now in college, they still return on weekends to help with the family business.

China Cafe is well known to residents of Napa and the surrounding area for its good food served in a stunning setting.

Speciallies

Baby Sweet Corn with Shrimp
Straw Mushrooms with Oyster Sauce
Almond Chicken Ding
Gai Kow: Chicken, mushrooms, bamboo shoots, sweet peas, and water chestnuts.
Ginger Beef
Curry Beef
Almond Duck: Duck served with sweet and sour sauce and garnished with crushed almonds.

MENU #1

China Cafe Special Chow Mein

Beef Chow Yuk *or* Sweet Pea Chow Yuk (seasonal)

Shrimp with Lobster Sauce

Almond Duck

Steamed Rice

MENU #2

Pork Won Ton

Almond Chicken Ding

Ginger Beef *or* Gai Kow

Green Vegetable Chow Yuk

Steamed Rice

MENU #3

Fried Prawns

Straw Mushrooms in Oyster Sauce

Paper-wrapped Chicken

Pineapple Barbecued Pork with Sweet and Sour Sauce

Ginger Beef

Steamed Rice

THE GOLDEN DRAGON $

1012 First Street (near Main)
Napa
Telephone: (707) 255-2446
Cuisine: Cantonese and American

Hours:
    11:30 A.M.–3:00 P.M., Monday, Wednesday–Saturday
    2:00 P.M.–9:00 P.M., Sunday

Credit cards: MC, Visa
Beer and wine only
City parking next door

    Located right downtown, The Golden Dragon is a favorite eating spot for business people, shoppers, and long-time Napa residents. A very charming, energetic couple, the Albert Lees, have owned this establishment for many years. They take such pride and joy in their restaurant that you'll feel like a guest enjoying Mr. Lee's home-style cooking (generous portions are served and little MSG is used).

    The Golden Dragon's chow mein is excellent. The noodles are pan-fried in a wok with such perfect timing that they brown evenly without burning. A very fine balance of meat, vegetables, and gravy is mixed with the noodles.

    During the dinner hours and on weekends, the Lees' children are usually at the restaurant serving guests or cleaning up. The Golden

Dragon is impeccably clean, spacious, and air-conditioned—an excellent family dining spot.

Specialties

Wor Won Ton
Chicken Chow Mein
Tomato Beef Chow Mein
Gai Kow: Mushrooms, bamboo shoots, sweet peas, chicken, and water chestnuts.
Curry Chicken
Curry Prawns
Shrimp in Lobster Sauce

Menu #1

Wor Won Ton

Chicken Chow Mein

Gai Kow

Goo Loo Yuk (sweet and sour pork)

Lychee Chicken

Steamed Rice

Menu #2

Tomato Beef Chow Mein

Green Vegetable Chow Yuk *or* Sweet Pea Pods (seasonal)

Pineapple Chicken

Ginger Beef

Jee Bow Gai (marinated chicken wrapped in foil and deep-fried)

Steamed Rice

Menu #3

Curry Prawns

Gai Ding Yee Mein (deep-fried noodles with chicken meat and vegetables in broth)

Almond Duck (served with sweet and sour sauce and garnished with crushed almonds)

Oyster Sauce Beef

Mushroom Chop Suey (mushrooms with vegetables in oyster sauce)

Steamed Rice

WONG'S RESTAURANT $$

1675 Trancas Street (near Jefferson)
Napa
Telephone: (707) 224-8507
Cuisine: Cantonese and American

Hours:
> 11:30 A.M.–2:00 P.M., 4:00 P.M.–9:00 P.M., Tuesday–Saturday
> noon–9:00 P.M., Sunday

Credit cards: AE, MC, Visa
Wine and beer only
Free parking lot

The distinctive tile roof of Wong's Restaurant resembles those found on many large homes in China. This spacious, air-conditioned establishment is tastefully decorated with Oriental decor and family heirlooms. The owners, the Owyeong family, designed the interior themselves, laying the carpets, hanging the wallpaper, and decorating everything down to the smallest detail.

The Owyeongs have been in business in Napa for over twenty years, four of which have been in their present location. Located on the north side of town, off Highway 28, the restaurant is popular with both locals and visitors. On weekends and busy days, Mr. Owyeong's two sons assist him with the cooking, while wife, Mary, and college-student daughter, Caroline, mind the cash register.

Do try Mr. Owyeong's Chinese long beans with beef when they are in season. Mr. Owyeong grows them in his garden, so they are always tender and fresh.

Specialties

Hong Kong Roast Duck (order one day in advance)
Hong Kong Steamed Chicken: Chicken, Chinese sausage, red dates, two
    kinds of mushrooms, and green onions, seasoned with a special sauce.
Wong's Steak Cubes
Beef with Chinese Long Beans (seasonal)
Lobster with Black Bean Sauce
Pineapple Sweet and Sour Shrimp
Abalone with Black Mushrooms: Sliced abalone and Chinese mushrooms
    simmered in oyster sauce.

MENU #1

Pork Won Ton

Chinese Green Vegetable

Abalone in Oyster Sauce

Cantonese Chicken Salad

Chicken with Black Mushrooms

Steamed Rice

MENU #2

Wong's Steak Cubes *or* Beef in Oyster Sauce

Pineapple Sweet and Sour Pork

Diced Almond Chicken

Almond Duck (served with sweet and sour sauce and garnished with crushed
    almonds)

Steamed Rice

MENU #3

Spring Egg Rolls

Wong's Fried Rice

Tomato Beef

Pineapple Sweet and Sour Shrimp

Beef with Green Peppers *or* Beef with Chinese Long Beans (seasonal)

SOUTH BAY

CHEF CHU'S $$

1067 North San Antonio Road (at El Camino Real)
Los Altos
Telephone: (415) 948-2696
Cuisine: Cantonese and Mandarin

Hours:
    11:30 A.M.–9:30 P.M., Monday–Thursday; until 10:00 P.M., Friday
    noon–10:00 P.M., Saturday
    noon–9:30 P.M., Sunday

Credit cards: MC, Visa
Full bar
Parking in rear

If you haven't heard of Chef Chu's you should know about this fine restaurant. It attracts people from miles away and it's always busy. A good selection of Mandarin dishes appears on the menu, as well as some Cantonese favorites. Almost every dish is excellently and consistently prepared. Lawrence Chu, chef and owner, has worked in other well-known Bay Area restaurants, including his father's, the first Mandarin restaurant on the peninsula. He travels to the Orient and dines out frequently to discover new dishes, then trains his cooks in their preparation.

There is an exciting interplay of contrasting and complementary ingredients, flavors, and textures in the dishes created by chef Chu. For example, the minced chicken with lettuce in which minced chicken, pork, black mushrooms, bamboo shoots, and water chestnuts are stir-fried with a dark seasoning sauce, then topped with a crust of almonds. You then fold a tablespoon of this mixture into a crisp lettuce leaf. In lover's prawns, two distinct flavors blend together when a wine sauce and a hot sauce are combined. In hot and sour beef, Hunan style, slices of beef are stir-fried with chili paste, minced garlic, and ginger, then poured over broccoli spears. Other specialties here are honey spareribs, pork with imperial sauce, crispy spicy duck, and smoked tea duck. A lunch-time favorite is the Mandarin chow mein.

Chef Chu and his staff will make your dining experience a pleasant one. Meals can be cooked to your specific needs—no MSG can be requested, as well as your preference on spiciness. For such outstanding food and service, the prices are moderate.

Specialties

Garlic Spicy Chicken: Steamed chicken served cold.
Crispy Spicy Duck: Seasoned, deep-fried duck served with steamed buns.
Chicken in Phoenix Nest: Slivers of taro root pressed into the shape of a basket and deep-fried, then filled with shrimp, snow peas, bamboo shoots, celery, water chestnuts, and mushrooms.
Steak Cubes
Hot Braised Whole Fish

Menu #1

Crispy Spicy Duck

Steak Cubes

Chef Chu's Lover's Prawns (prawns in a special spicy sauce)

Vegetable Delight (snow peas, black mushrooms, and bamboo shoots)

Mu Shu Pork

Steamed rice

Menu #2

Three Delight Sizzling Rice Soup (shrimp, abalone, and chicken in a chicken broth, served "sizzling" with deep-fried rice patties)

Honey Barbecued Spareribs

Chicken in Phoenix Nest

Garlic Spicy Chicken

Hot Braised Whole Fish

Steamed Rice

Menu #3

Shredded Chicken Salad

Potstickers

Mandarin Chow Mein (black mushrooms, shrimp, barbecued pork, and chicken with pan-fried noodles)

Szechuan Beef (served over deep-fried rice-stick noodles)

Chinese Peas with Water Chestnuts

CHINA HOUSE $$

2507 South El Camino Real (near 25th)
San Mateo
Telephone: (415) 574-9760
Cuisine: Cantonese

Hours:
    11:30 A.M.–9:30 P.M., Tuesday–Sunday

No credit cards
Reservations advised

    Driving along El Camino Real near the Hillsdale Shopping Center, you are sure to see China House, a bright, Chinese-style, yellow building with a green tile roof. The dining room, pleasantly decorated with Chinese folk art pictures and lacquer furniture, has a quiet, restful ambience.

    The specialty of the house is suey gow, minced pork dumplings, served in a number of ways. They are fried and served as appetizers, or afloat in a delicate broth. The hon sea suey gow mein is stir-fried noodles and vegetables with fried suey gow and a delicious gravy. To our knowledge, China House is the only restaurant that serves this latter dish.

    Many dishes popular in San Francisco's Chinatown can be ordered here. The chef-owner worked at a restaurant in San Francisco before opening this one. His wife and children help in the kitchen and with the serving of the food.

Specialties

Hon Sea Suey Gow Mein: Pork dumplings are first deep-fried, then a mixture of meat, vegetables, and noodles are stir-fried and placed on top of them.

Suey Gow Soup: Pork Dumpling soup.

Fried Suey Gow: Deep-fried pork dumpling.
Cantonese Chicken Salad
Grilled Prawns with Bacon (butterfly prawns)
Steak Cubes

MENU #1

Suey Gow Soup

Cantonese Chicken Salad

Prawns with Black Bean Sauce

Snow Peas with Beef

Steamed Rice

MENU #2

Abalone Soup

Fried Suey Gow

Chicken with Black Mushrooms

Broccoli with Pork

Tomato Beef

Steamed Rice

MENU #3

Hon Sea Suey Gow Mein

Grilled Prawns with Bacon

Abalone with Oyster Sauce

Steak Cubes with Chinese Greens

Steamed Rice

CHOPSTICKS $

360 Castro Street
Mountain View
Telephone: (415) 969-0500
Cuisine: Cantonese and Mandarin

Hours:
    11:00 A.M.–9:00 P.M., Wednesday–Monday

Credit cards: MC, Visa
Full bar
Reservations needed for six or more

There are may reasons for the popularity of this comfortable, reasonably priced, chef-owned restaurant in Mountain View. The choicest, most tender vegetables are served, cooked to a shiny, crunchy finish. The seafood is always fresh and well prepared. Specialties popular in many San Francisco restaurants and delicatessens, such as crispy chicken, roast duck, and chicken stuffed with sweet rice, are equally good at Chopsticks.

The chow fun noodle dish we ordered for lunch one day was evenly browned in the wok, with a good balance of beef, greens, bean sprouts, and green onions. We'd also like to pass on a tip! The selection on the menu doesn't truly represent the vegetable dishes this restaurant is capable of creating. Ask the waiter what fresh vegetables are available, then ask him for preparation suggestions. For example, the stir-fried asparagus with beef is absolutely delicious.

Though Cantonese dishes dominate the menu, Mandarin ones are also available. The management of Chopsticks will be happy to assist you in planning a banquet or special dinner.

Specialties

Clams Sautéed in Garlic Sauce
Steamed Fresh Cod
Roast Duck
Chopsticks Lobster: Stir-fried cubes of fresh lobster meat, snow peas, mushrooms, water chestnuts, and vegetables.
Asparagus Sautéed in Black Bean Sauce

MENU #1

Winter Melon Soup

Clams Sautéed in Garlic Sauce

Roast Duck

Asparagus Chicken (seasonal) *or* Chicken with Tender Greens

Chopsticks Special Steak Cubes

Steamed Rice

MENU #2

Sizzling Rice Soup

Snow Pea Beef

Steamed Fresh Cod

Chopsticks Lobster

Steamed Rice

MENU #3

Pork Spareribs with Black Bean Sauce

Stir-fried Rock Cod with Chinese Greens

Spareribs Sautéed in Black Bean Sauce

Black Mushrooms and Abalone

Pan-fried Prawns in Shells

Steamed Rice

FUNG LUM $$

1815 S. Bascom Avenue (near Prune Yard Shopping Center)
San Jose
Telephone: (408) 277-6955
Cuisine: Cantonese and Mandarin

Hours:
    11:30 A.M.–2:00 P.M., 5:00 P.M.–10:00 P.M., Monday–Sunday
    5:00 P.M.–10:30 P.M., Saturday
    noon–9:00 P.M., Sunday

Credit cards, MC, Visa
Full bar
Free parking lot

Enter the palace and be served food fit for royalty. Outside the gates is busy Bascom Avenue, but walk through the large, ornate doors of Fung Lum restaurant and quiet elegance awaits you. Everything inside has been handmade—the decorative ceilings, furniture, brass and wood carvings,

Oriental carpets. The owners, the Pang family, special ordered the furnishings in Taipei and even brought over a crew to assemble the artifacts in the restaurant.

The large, sunken dining room is surround by a terrace. Two-thousand-year-old Chinese designs adorn the large, brass-plated columns and beams. Oriental folk art is displayed throughout the building. Notice the hand-painted glass plates on each of the four sides of the brass lanterns hanging from the ceiling. In one corner of the restaurant, cross over the bridge and view the miniature waterfall. There are also two private dining rooms that are truly elegant.

You can watch the large kitchen in action through windows constructed for this purpose. On one side is the area where food is washed and cut. Then it is passed across a long table, with middlemen handing each of the six cooks the ingredients in their order of use. Once the dishes are cooked, there are four bus boys waiting to take the food to the tables immediately. Manager Daniel Pang stresses that there are six cooks to insure proper timing for each dish.

Given the beauty of the setting and the care that goes into the preparation of each dish, you will be amazed at how moderate the prices are. Daniel Pang sums up his thoughts about his family's restaurant this way: "Each dish must look good, smell good, and taste good at Fung Lum." It is no wonder so many people come here from as far away as San Francisco and Sacramento to dine.

Specialties

Skewered Beef Saday: Beef marinated in special saday sauce and broiled on bamboo skewers.
Mini Spring Roll
Creamed Corn Soup: One of the most popular soups in the Taipei branch of Fung Lum restaurant.
Minced Squab
Fung Lum Special Spareribs: Deep-fried spareribs with sweet and sour sauce.
Sweet and Sour Pork

MENU #1
Skewered Beef Saday

Creamed Corn Soup

Salt-baked Prawns (pan-fried prawns with special flavored salt)

Fung Lum Special Lemon Chicken
Fung Lum Special Spareribs
Tender Greens in Oyster Sauce
Steamed Rice

MENU #2
Mini Spring Rolls
West Lake Minced Beef Soup
Crispy Skin Chicken
Skewered Beef Saday
Bean Curd Szechuan Style (spicy)
Steamed Rice

MENU #3
Minced Squab
Shrimp with Cashew Nuts
Sweet and Sour Pork
Baked Chicken in Black Bean Sauce
Beef with Snow Peas
Steamed Rice

KEE JOON'S $$$

433 Airport Boulevard
Burlingame
Telephone: (415) 348-1122
Cuisine: Cantonese and Mandarin

Hours:
   11:30 A.M.–2:00 P.M., Monday–Friday
   5:00 P.M.–10:00 P.M., Sunday–Thursday
   5:00 P.M.–10:30 P.M., Friday–Saturday

Credit cards: AE, BC, MC
Full bar and extensive wine list
Reservations recommended for four or more
Parking under building

When you leave the underground garage and ascend to the penthouse, you are transported to the era of the Sung Dynasty and to Kee Joon's. Wooden panels accented with gilt hand carvings fill the foyer, in the center of which is a large marble fountain. Magnificent views can be seen from every room of the glass-enclosed penthouse.

The service here is outstanding, and each dish is a gastronomic accomplishment. Complementary flavors and contrasting textures blend together so well that table seasonings are unnecessary. As our party of eight sat down, a waiter took each napkin from the table and placed it on a diner's lap. Each course was announced, shown to the table, and then served individually to each diner (even some accompanying sauces and condiments were served with only one course). Courses were served piping hot at ten-minute intervals, the plates were collected after each, and a clean, warm one was left for the next course.

The prices here are expensive, as they are at other restaurants of this caliber, but they are worth it for the outstanding service, good food, magnificent views, and Sung Dynasty decor.

Specialties

Stuffed King Crab Legs: Boned crab legs stuffed with crab meat, mushrooms, green onions, water chestnuts, and pork, and served with a delicate sauce.
Peking Steamed Dumpling: Very thin dough stuffed with ground pork, green onions, and bamboo shoots, then steamed.
Sizzling Rice Soup
Mu Shu Pork
Hang Yung Chicken: Marinated cubes of chicken with almond paste, panfried to a crispy golden brown.
Mongolian Lamb

Menu #1
Sizzling Rice Soup
Stuffed King Crab Legs
Mixed Vegetable Sauté

Hang Yung Chicken
Szechuan Spiced Beef
Steamed Rice

MENU #2
Peking Steamed Dumplings
Cantonese Chicken Salad (sai see gai)
Scallops Cantonese
Mu Shu Pork
Stir-fried Snow Peas
Steamed Rice

MENU #3
Butterfly Prawns
Crab Meat Winter Melon Soup
Triple Mushrooms with Oyster Sauce (black, straw, and button mushrooms)
Lemon Chicken
Manchurian Beef (cubes of beef marinated in special sauce, stir-fried with onion
    and green pepper)
Steamed Rice

MUI KIANG $$

895 Villa Street
Mountain View
Telephone: (415) 979-8232
Cuisine: Hakka

Hours:
    11:30 A.M.–2:00 P.M., Sunday–Friday
    5:00 P.M.–9:30 P.M., Sunday–Thursday
    5:00 P.M.–10:30 P.M., Friday and Saturday

Credit cards: AE, DC, MC, Visa
Full bar
Reservations recommended on weekends
Free parking lot

The Hakka people, who occupy the tranquil countryside outside the city of Hong Kong, are known for their peaceful, gentle ways, and this is reflected in their cuisine. Hakka-style cooking is similar to Cantonese, only the food is more subtle in taste and delicate in flavorings. A charming Hakka family has opened a spacious restaurant to share its cuisine with South Bay residents. The Tse family still maintains two Hakka restaurants by the same name in Hong Kong, and special Hakka sauces and ingredients are sent in by air from Hong Kong.

One of the most unusual dishes served here is angel's treat, balls of milk and chicken broth whipped to a custard and then dropped by tablespoons into hot oil. This creation is crispy on the outside and soft, moist, and deliciously flavored on the inside. Another unusual culinary delight is beef ball soup. Finely chopped beef is mixed with a small amount of water and salt and then whipped at high speed to form a light, airy mixture. This mixture is formed into balls and served in a delicate beef broth garnished with green onions.

The spacious, comfortable atmosphere at Mui Kiang will make your dining experience pleasant. Many Cantonese dishes are also on the menu, but with the "Hakka touch."

Specialties

Hakka Chow Mein: Fried noodles with bamboo shoots, mushrooms, green onions, bean sprouts, and pork, served with a delicate sauce.
Mui Kiang Shredded Scallops: A traditional Hakka delicacy prepared with costly, imported dried scallops, black mushrooms, bamboo shoots, and fluffed eggs.
Vegetables with Mixed Mushrooms: Seasonal vegetables covered with Chinese, straw, and button mushrooms, stir-fried in oyster sauce.
Angel's Treat: A delicate appetizer made with chicken and pork flavorings, crispy on the outside and soft on the inside.
Beef Ball Soup: Lean beef balls in a delicious beef broth, garnished with chopped green onions.

Menu #1

Mui Kiang Special Beef Soup

Fried Rock Cod Fillet in Creamed Corn Sauce

Mui Kiang Salt-baked Chicken

Vegetables with Mixed Mushrooms (seasonal)

Beef with Snow Peas

Steamed Rice

Menu #2

Mui Kiang Shredded Scallops *or* Mui Kiang Braised Bean Curd

Lotus Blossom Beef (cubes of beef, stir-fried with seasonal vegetables)

Mui Kiang Fried Spareribs

Pressed Duck with Imperial Taro (boned, deep-fried duck topped with a layer of
  taro and served with mushroom sauce)

Steamed Rice

Menu #3

Stir-fried Scallops

Fried Rock Cod Fillet in Sweet and Sour Sauce *or* Steamed Whole Fresh Rock
  Cod (seasonal)

Diced Chicken in Hot and Spicy Sauce

Tender Greens in Oyster Sauce

Steamed Rice

PIERRE'S (The Wah Yen Restaurant) $$

211 South San Mateo Drive
San Mateo
Telephone: (415) 343-1144
Cuisine: Cantonese and Mandarin

Hours:
> 11:00 A.M.–9:00 P.M., Monday–Saturday

Credit cards: MC, Visa
Beer and Wine only
Reservations recommended

Turn people away rather than expand and lose control: this has been the decision of the K. K. Leongs, owners of this fine, small, family-run restaurant in downtown San Mateo. Eva Leong, the cook at Pierre's, comments, "We love to cook and enjoy seeing our customers come back often. We don't want to make too much money; we just want to keep the good quality and use the best ingredients for our customers."

Tender, loving care is evident in all of the dishes served at Pierre's. For even a simple dish such as Chinese Greens with Oyster Sauce, only the choicest, most tender parts of bok choy are used. Potstickers are made with homemade dough and stuffed with a combination of ingredients that is distinctively Pierre's. In Beef Steaks Chinese Style, slices of tender beef are marinated in a most unique sauce.

For lunch, try any of the won ton soup dishes. Some people swear the won tons here are the best! Chicken Fried Noodles are another hit with many of the regular patrons.

Incidentally, Pierre's was a popular French restaurant. The Leongs decided to keep the name since it was associated with fine food. However, to the many Chinese patrons, it's known as the Wah Yen Restaurant.

Be sure to call in advance for a reservation; otherwise you may be one of the many turned away.

Specialties

Silver-Wrapped Chicken: Chicken chunk marinated in special sauce and deep-fried.

Mandarin Pressed Duck: Crisp fried boneless duck masked with sweet and sour sauce and sprinkled with chopped almond.

Beef Steaks Chinese Style: Slices of tender beef marinated with distinctive sauce and toss cooked.

Chicken Fried Noodles: Pan-fried noodles, mixed vegetables with sliced chicken.

MENU # 1

Silver-Wrapped Chicken

Chicken Fried Noodles

Wor Won Ton (Won ton cooked with mushrooms, bamboo shoots, vegetables, barbecued pork, and shrimps in chicken broth)

Chinese Greens with Oyster Sauce

Steamed Rice

MENU # 2

Potstickers

Gulf Prawns with Black Bean Sauce

Beef Steaks Chinese Style

Bean Cake with Pork Minced

Steamed Rice

MENU # 3

Scallop Soup (One day advance notice required) (Scallop broth with shreds of chicken, bamboo shoots, and egg blossom)

Mandarin Pressed Duck

Szechuan Pork

Beef Steaks Chinese Style

Steamed Rice

THE POT STICKER $$

3708 South El Camino Real (near 37th)
San Mateo
Telephone: (415) 349-0149
Cuisine: Mandarin

Hours:
   11:30 A.M.–2:00 P.M., Monday–Friday
   4:30 P.M.–9:30 P.M., daily

Credit cards: MC, Visa
Beer and wine only
Reservations needed for six or more
Parking in rear

    In 1973, The Pot Sticker opened three blocks south of the Hillsdale Shopping Center. It became so well known that many people drove to it from San Francisco. To satisfy these long-distance patrons, a Pot Sticker was opened in San Francisco on Waverly Place (page 71).
    The San Mateo Pot Sticker is much more spacious than the San Francisco restaurant. Most of the savory dishes at the San Francisco branch can be ordered here, too, except for a few Chinese favorites, such as chicken gizzards with pork and bean curd pork. Such gastronomic delights as beggar's chicken, Peking duck, and crispy fish can be ordered only at the San Mateo location. The suggested menus and specialties are much the same as at the San Francisco branch, with these few exceptions.

SZECHUAN VILLAGE $$

427 Gellert Boulevard
Daly City
Telephone: (415) 992-2444
Cuisine: Szechuan

Hours:
    11:30 A.M.–10:00 P.M., daily

Credit cards: MC, Visa
Reservations advised

    Szechuan Village is a pleasant, spacious neighborhood restaurant, with wooden paneling, grass-patterned wallpaper, and Chinese screen and brush paintings. If you enjoy hot, spicy Chinese food, you'll like many of the dishes served here.
    The suggested menus and specialties are the same as at the Szechuan Village in Pleasant Hill (page 116).

TAO TAO   **$$**

175 South Murphy Avenue
Sunnyvale
Telephone: (408) 736-3731
Cuisine: Cantonese

Hours:
   11:00 A.M.–2:00 P.M., Monday –Friday
   4:00 P.M.–10:00 P.M., Monday–Saturday
   4:00 P.M.–9:30 P.M., Sunday

Credit cards: AE, BA, MC
Full bar

This air-conditioned, family-style establishment is very modern, with a large bar in the middle of the restaurant and spacious, low-lit dining rooms on both sides of it. There is a special lunch menu for the business and shopping crowd, but if you happen to drop in at noon and feel like ordering other than the standard dishes on this menu, ask to see the "take-out" menu and order from it.

This is a popular spot for travelers from the Carmel-Monterey area and for the Chinese who come here and order their favorite dishes, many of which do not appear on the regular menu.

Specialties

Pine Nut Shrimp or Chicken: Shrimp or chicken with pine nuts, yellow
   onion, celery, water chestnuts, and peas; not listed on the menu.
Sesame Chicken: Deep-fried chicken pieces, garnished with toasted sesame
   seeds.
Cantonese Chicken Salad
Tao Tao Beef: Sliced beef stir-fried with hoisin sauce.
Mongolian Beef

Lunch Menu Recommendations

Tao Tao Chicken Wings
Chicken Salad
Beef Rice Noodles

Barbecued Spareribs
Tao Tao Special Chow Mein
Gorn Low Won Ton: Won ton in oyster sauce.
Wor Won Ton

MENU #1

Cantonese Chicken Salad

Abalone Soup

Tao Tao Beef

Shrimp with Lobster Sauce

Stir-fried Chinese Greens

Steamed Rice

MENU #2

Tao Tao Chicken Wings

Bird's Nest Soup

Pine Nut Chicken *or* Pine Nut Shrimp

Steak Cubes with Chinese Greens

Sesame Chicken

Vegetables under Snow (vegetables topped with deep-fried rice-stick noodles)

Steamed Rice

MENU #3

Wor Won Ton Soup

Mongolian Beef

Shrimp with Lobster Sauce

Chicken with Chinese Mushrooms

Steamed Whole Fish

Steamed Rice

WING FAT $

500 East Third Avenue
San Mateo
Telephone: (415) 344-0757
Cuisine: Cantonese

Hours:
10:00 A.M.–8:00 P.M., Tuesday–Sunday

Wing Fat is a small, unpretentious eating spot that has exceptionally good food. Located in the older section of downtown San Mateo, it attracts many long-time locals.

Such home-style Chinese favorites as black bean sauce spareribs, kau yuk (stewed pork belly), and sin choy (pickled sweet and sour cabbage) are always available at Wing Fat. Chef Tom Leong's barbecued spareribs and roast pork are lean, juicy, and perfect in flavor. If you happen to be here when these meats are still warm from the oven, the enticing aroma will be almost overwhelming. Mr. Leong proudly commented on another dish. "One of the most popular items here is fried rice, because we add more meat and eggs to ours than in most other places, and that's how our patrons like it."

Wing Fat is definitely a "no-frills" restaurant. This family-run eatery has efficient, attentive service and reasonable prices. If you don't have the time to eat at Wing Fat, do what many locals do and order the food by phone to take home.

Specialties

Barbecued Spareribs
Barbecued Pork
Beef Chow Fun
Ginger Beef
Lop Chong: Steamed Chinese sausage.
Beef Stew
Barbecued Pork Fried Rice

MENU #1

Abalone Soup
Barbecued Spareribs *or* Barbecued Pork

Ginger Beef
Spareribs with Black Bean Sauce
Steamed Rice

Menu #2
Beef Chow Fun
Shrimp with Chinese Greens
Cashew Nut Chicken
Oyster Sauce with Beef
Steamed Rice

Menu #3
Wor Won Ton Soup
Roast Duck (order a half duck)
Shrimp with Lobster Sauce
Barbecued Pork Fried Rice
Lop Chong

YAT SING $$

327 First Street (near San Antonio)
Los Altos
Telephone: (415) 948-3393
Cuisine: Mandarin

Hours:
    11:00 A.M.–9:00 P.M., Monday–Friday
    4:00 P.M.–9:00 P.M., Saturday

Credit cards: BA, MC

A former chef from the famous, San Francisco-based Yet Wah establishments has opened an attractive, comfortable, family-style restaurant in Los Altos. Yat Sing is conveniently located a short distance from Highway 101. The restaurant is immaculate and very spacious, and the extensive menu is predominantly Mandarin with a few Cantonese dishes. Chef James Ko has good intuition in blending flavors and textures.

Dine in an unhurried atmosphere with a friendly staff who will be delighted to assist you in ordering your meal.

Specialties

Cantonese Chicken Salad (not listed on the menu)
Potstickers
Su Mi: Fried pork dumplings.
Sizzling Rice Soup
Mongolian Beef *or* Lamb
Boneless Sweet and Sour Stuffed Chicken Wings: Boned wings stuffed with pork, chicken meat, mushrooms, water chestnuts, and bamboo shoots, served with sweet and sour sauce.

Menu #1

Potstickers

Cantonese Chicken Salad

Szechuan Spiced Beef

Mongolian Lamb *or* Boneless Sweet and Sour Stuffed Chicken Wings

Scallops with Mixed Vegetables

Steamed Rice

Menu #2

Sizzling Rice Soup

Su Mi

Boneless Sweet and Sour Stuffed Chicken Wings

Mu Shu Pork

Lobster Meat with Black Bean Sauce *or* Whole Crab with Black Bean Sauce (seasonal)

Steamed Rice

Menu #3

Shrimp Roll *or* Potstickers
Hot and Sour Soup
Beef with Broccoli *or* Steak Cubes with Chinese Greens
Kung Pao Chicken
Black Mushrooms with Chinese Greens
Steamed Rice

RECIPES FROM THE RESTAURANTS

Almond Beef with Broccoli

$^1/_3$ pound sirloin of beef
$^1/_2$ bunch broccoli
$^1/_4$ cup vegetable oil
$^1/_4$ cup chicken broth or water
$^1/_2$ cup toasted almonds

Marinade
1 tablespoon soy sauce
$^1/_2$ teaspoon sugar
1 teaspoon cornstarch
$^1/_4$ teaspoon garlic powder
2 tablespoons white wine

Thinly slice the beef into 2-inch-long pieces. Combine all of the ingredients for the marinade and add the sliced beef. Set aside for 30 minutes.

Cut the broccoli spears into 2-inch lengths, then cut each piece into 4 lengthwise strips. Bring a saucepan of water to a boil and add the broccoli. Cook for 5 minutes, uncovered. Remove from the heat, drain, and immerse the broccoli in cold water for about 5 minutes. Drain well and set broccoli aside.

Heat a wok until very hot and add the oil. When the oil is hot, stir-fry the beef and its marinade until it is cooked. Remove the beef with a slotted utensil and set aside. Add the broccoli to the oil and juice remaining in the wok and stir-fry 3 minutes. Then add the chicken broth or water, cover, and bring to a boil. Add the beef, stir-fry about 1 minute, and remove to a serving plate. Strew almonds over the top and serve immediately.

Kee Joon's
433 Airport Boulevard
Burlingame

Beggar's Chicken

One 3-pound fryer chicken
1 tablespoon sherry
1$^1/_2$ teaspoons salt
$^1/_2$ teaspoon five-spice powder
$^1/_2$ teaspoon Oriental sesame oil
$^1/_2$ teaspoon soy sauce

Stuffing
3 water chestnuts, sliced
3 to 4 slices Virginia ham, cut in julienne
4 or 5 dried Chinese black mushrooms, soaked in water to soften, drained, and sliced
20 thin slices bamboo shoot, cut in julienne

Sauce
1 cup chicken broth
1 tablespoon cottonseed oil
1 tablespoon sherry
$^1/_2$ teaspoon sugar
Dash of msg
1 tablespoon soy sauce
1 tablespoon oyster sauce
Few drops of Oriental sesame oil
2 teaspoons cornstarch, mixed with 2 tablespoons water

Wash the chicken and pat it dry. Rub the cavity and outside of chicken with sherry. Combine the salt, five-spice powder, sesame oil, and soy sauce and rub this mixture in the cavity and on the outside of the chicken. Combine all of the stuffing ingredients, fill the chicken cavity, and secure it closed.

Preheat the oven to 450°F. Wrap the chicken in two layers of aluminum foil and then place it in a brown paper bag that fits it snugly. Secure the bag closed. Mix dry ceramic clay (available in art-supply stores) with water until it is a thick, spreadable consistency and completely cover the bag with a 1/4-inch-thick layer of it. Place the clay-encased chicken on a baking sheet and put it into the preheated oven. Bake for 1½ hours, then reduce temperature to 300°F and bake for an additional 45 minutes.

Just before the chicken is finished baking, combine all of the ingredients for the sauce in a saucepan and cook for several minutes over medium heat until it is fairly thick. Remove the chicken from the oven, and with a mallet, crack the clay and pull away the paper. The meat should be falling from the bones. Ladle the sauce over the chicken just before serving.

The Mandarin
900 North Point
San Francisco

Chicken Salad Cantonese

One 3-pound fryer chicken
1¹/₂ cups water
1 quart vegetable oil for deep-frying
¹/₂ cup raw peanuts
3 ounces rice-stick noodles (*py mei fun*)
¹/₄ cup raw sesame seeds
1 tablespoon vegetable oil
3 stalks celery, cut in 2-inch lengths and then into julienne
3 green onions, slivered
Sugar and salt to taste
¹/₄ head lettuce, shredded

Spice mixture for chicken
1 teaspon salt
¹/₂ teaspoon sugar
1 teaspoon thin soy sauce
1 teaspoon oyster sauce
¹/₄ teaspoon five-spice powder

Spice mixture for salad
¹/₂ teaspoon dry mustard
1 teaspoon water
¹/₂ teaspoon sugar
1 teaspoon flavored salt (see Note)
2 teaspoons oyster sauce
1 tablespoon Oriental sesame oil

Wash the chicken and pat it dry. Combine all of the ingredients for the spice mixture for the chicken and rub the mixture in the cavity and on the outside of the fowl. Pour the water in a roasting pan, place a rack in the pan, and set the chicken on it. Roast in a preheated 375°F oven for 1 hour and 45 minutes, turning the chicken once to brown it on both sides and basting it several times. Remove the chicken from the oven and let it cool until it can be easily handled. Remove the skin from the chicken and cut it in julienne. Remove the meat from the bones and shred it by hand. Set the chicken meat and skin aside separately.

Heat the 1 quart of oil in a deep pan or wok to 325°F. Deep-fry the peanuts until golden brown, remove with a slotted utensil and drain well. Finely chop the peanuts and set them aside. In the same oil, deep-fry the rice-stick noodles, a small amount at a time, just until they puff and barely begin to change color. Remove with a slotted utensil and drain on paper toweling; set aside. Place the sesame seeds in a dry frying pan over low heat until golden brown, about 3 minutes. Remove from the frying pan and set aside.

Heat the 1 tablespoon vegetable oil in a wok and stir-fry the celery and green onions for about 3 minutes, sprinkling them lightly with sugar and salt. Remove from the wok and set aside.

To prepare the spice mixture for the salad, mix together the dry mustard and water and combine with the chicken meat. Add the sugar, flavored salt, oyster sauce, and sesame oil to the chicken meat and mix well. Then add the stir-fried vegetables, shredded lettuce, and chicken skin and mix well again. Just before serving, add the toasted nuts, sesame seeds and rice-stick noodles and toss lightly.

Note: To make flavored salt, heat 2 tablespoons salt in a dry frying pan placed over medium heat for 3 minutes. Remove from the heat, add 1 teaspoon five-spice powder and stir well. Store in a jar with a tightly fitting lid. This mixture will keep indefinitely.

Yat Sing
327 First Street
Los Altos

Chicken Walnut

2 tablespoons peanut oil
1 pound boneless chicken breast meat, cut in thin strips
1 teaspoon salt
$^1/_4$ cup snow peas
4 ounces small mushrooms
2 ounces sliced bamboo shoots
2 cups chicken broth
1 tablespoon soy sauce
$^1/_2$ teaspoon sugar
$1^1/_4$ cups toasted walnuts, coarsely chopped
$1^1/_2$ teaspoons cornstarch, mixed with 1 teaspoon water

Heat a wok until very hot and add the oil. When the oil is hot, add the chicken and salt and stir-fry for 2 to 3 minutes. Add the snow peas, mushrooms, bamboo shoots, and chicken broth, and continuing to stir-fry, cook for 2 minutes. Add the soy sauce, sugar, and walnuts, mix well, and stir in the cornstarch-water mixture. Cook, continuing to stir, just until pan juices are slightly thickened.

Imperial Palace
919 Grant Avenue
San Francisco

Chinese Doughnuts

1 pound glutinous rice powder
3 ounces sugar
3 ounces wheat starch
1¼ cups water
¼ cup raw sesame seeds
Vegetable oil for deep-frying

Filling
¼ cup toasted sesame seeds
1 cup roasted peanuts, finely chopped
3 ounces candied winter melon, diced
⅔ cup sweetened shredded coconut

Combine all of the ingredients for the filling, mix well, and set aside. In a mixing bowl, combine the rice powder, sugar, and wheat starch. Add the water, mixing it with the dry ingredients to form a smooth dough. Divide the dough into 20 equal-sized portions. Flatten each portion with the palm of your hand, make an indentation in the center and place ¾ tablespoon of the filling in the hollow. Bring the edges of the dough up around the filling to cover it completely and give the top a twist to seal it closed. When you have finished forming each doughnut, roll it in the sesame seeds.

When all of the doughnuts are formed, heat the oil in a deep pan or wok to 325°F. Gently drop the doughnuts, a few at a time, into the hot oil, being careful to keep them separated so that they do not stick together. After about 2 minutes, when the doughnuts have begun to brown and float, press each one into the oil several times with a Chinese wire strainer. This will make them puff. Continue cooking for approximately 6 more minutes. Remove with a slotted utensil and drain on paper toweling.

Canton Tea House
1108 Stockton Street
San Francisco

Crispy Chicken

4 quarts water
1 tablespoon salt
One 4-pound chicken
1 tablespoon honey
1 tablespoon five-spice powder
1 quart vegetable oil
1/2 lemon, cut in 3 wedges

Seasoning mixture
1 tablespoon vinegar
1 tablespoon wine
1 tablespoon soy sauce
2 tablespoons cornstarch
1 tablespoon honey
1 tablespoon sugar

Bring 2 quarts of the water to a boil in a large pot and add the salt. Tie a string around the neck of the chicken and immerse the chicken in the boiling water for 4 minutes. Pull the chicken from the water by the string. In a second large pot, bring the remaining 2 quarts of water to a boil and add the honey. Immerse the chicken in the water and cook for 6 minutes, then pull it from the water by the string. Combine all of the ingredients for the seasoning mixture in a small bowl, and with a pastry brush, coat the cavity and outside of the chicken with the mixture. Using the string, hang the chicken to air dry for 6 hours.

Heat the oil in a wok or large deep pan to 350°F. Deep-fry the whole chicken for approximately 25 minutes, or until the skin is golden brown. Remove the chicken from the oil and set it aside to cool. Cut the chicken into 2- by 1-inch pieces and place on a serving platter. Arrange the lemon wedges on the platter and serve.

Asia Garden
772 Pacific Avenue
San Francisco

Empress Beef

3 or 4 tablespoons vegetable oil
$^1/_2$ pound sirloin of beef, cut in long, thin strips
$^1/_4$ tablespoon salt
1 large white onion, thinly sliced
3 stalks celery, coarsely chopped
1 small can button mushrooms, drained and thinly sliced
$^1/_4$ pound snow peas, each cut once on the diagonal, or
 $^1/_4$ pound French-cut string beans
$^1/_2$ small can water chestnuts, coarsely chopped
1 tablespoon cornstarch
5 tablespoons soy sauce
$^1/_2$ tablespoon sugar
$^1/_2$ cup water

Heat a wok until very hot and add the oil. When the oil is hot, add the beef and salt and stir-fry until the beef is browned. Add the onion, celery, mushrooms, snow peas or string beans, and water chestnuts and gently stir-fry for a few minutes over high heat. Cover the pan, reduce heat, and simmer for about 3 minutes. Combine the cornstarch, soy sauce, sugar, and water, mix well, and add to the pan. Stir just until the pan juices have thickened slightly. Serve immediately.

Empress of China
838 Grant Avenue
San Francisco

Empress Egg Rolls

$^1/_4$ cup vegetable oil
4 ounces bamboo shoots, shredded
4 ounces dried Chinese black mushrooms, soaked in water to
  soften, drained, and slivered
3 stalks celery, cut in thin 1-inch long strips
1 medium onion, finely chopped
$^1/_2$ pound shelled, cooked prawns, cut in small pieces
1 pound bean sprouts
1 teaspoon salt
2 tablespoons sugar
$^1/_4$ cup soy sauce
8 egg roll skins (available in Chinese groceries and some
  supermarkets)
Vegetable oil for deep-frying
1 egg, beaten

Heat a wok until very hot and add the $^1/_4$ cup oil. When the oil is hot, add the bamboo shoots, mushrooms, celery, onion, prawns, bean sprouts, salt, sugar, and soy sauce and stir-fry until ingredients are half cooked. Remove from the pan and drain well. Divide the stir-fried mixture evenly among the 8 egg roll skins and roll each up to form a tube 1 inch in diameter.

Heat the oil in a wok or deep pan to 325°F. Dip each egg roll in the beaten egg and deep-fry in the hot oil until golden brown, cooking only a few at a time so as not to crowd them in the pan. Remove from the oil with a slotted utensil and drain well. To serve, cut each egg roll into 4 pieces.

Empress of China
838 Grant Avenue
San Francisco

Fried Dumplings (Potstickers)

$2^{1}/_{2}$ cups all-purpose flour
$^{2}/_{3}$ cup boiling water
1 cup cold water
3 tablespoons vegetable oil

Filling
$^{3}/_{4}$ pound ground pork
4 ounces raw shrimp, shelled and cut in small pieces
3 dried Chinese black mushrooms, soaked in water to soften,
    drained, and chopped
1 tablespoon chopped green onion
1 teaspoon chopped ginger root
2 tablespoons soy sauce
2 teaspoons salt
2 tablespoons Oriental sesame oil or melted and cooled lard
10 ounces cabbage or spinach

Put the flour in a mixing bowl, add boiling water, and mix with chopsticks. Add $^{1}/_{3}$ cup of the cold water, mix in to form a dough, and knead until smooth and elastic. Cover with a tea towel and let stand 15 minutes.

To make the filling, combine the pork, shrimp, mushrooms, green onion, ginger, soy sauce, salt, and sesame oil or lard in a bowl and mix thoroughly. Bring a saucepan of water to a boil, add the cabbage or spinach, and cook for about 3 minutes. Remove from the heat, drain well, and immerse in cold water. Drain well again, squeezing as much water from the leaves as possible, and chop finely. Squeeze dry again and add to the pork mixture, mixing well.

Remove the dough to a lightly floured board and knead again until smooth. Divide the dough into 40 equal-sized pieces. Working quickly so the dough does not dry out, flatten each piece with the palm of your hand, and then roll it out into a $2^{1}/_{2}$-inch round. Place 1 tablespoon of filling in the center of each round and fold over to make a half-moon shape, pinching edges together securely. Very carefully, stretch each half-moon shape so that it is slightly longer.

Heat a frying pan until very hot and add 2 tablespoons of the oil. When the oil is hot, arrange as many dumplings as possible in the pan in a flower pattern, making sure the dumplings are not touching (about 20 dumplings in a 10-inch pan). Fry the dumplings until they are golden on the bottom, about 1 minute, then add the remaining ⅔ cup water, cover the pan, and cook until the water has evaporated. Add the remaining 1 tablespoon of oil at the edge of the pan and fry, uncovered, for 30 seconds. Place a serving plate over the pan and invert the pan quickly so that the dumplings maintain the flower pattern. Repeat the cooking procedure with the remaining dumplings, keeping the already cooked ones warm in the oven.

Asia Palace
885–887 Fourth Street
San Rafael

Half-Moon Dumplings

1 pound wheat starch
2½ cups boiling water

Filling
3 ounces dried Chinese black mushrooms, soaked in water to soften and drained
3 ounces raw prawns, shelled and deveined
½ pound lean pork butt

3 ounces bamboo shoots
2 ounces carrot, peeled
1 teaspoon salt
$^1/_2$ teaspoon sugar
1 tablespoon Oriental sesame oil
1 tablespoon soy sauce
2 tablespoons cornstarch
Dash of black pepper

Put the wheat starch in a mixing bowl, add the boiling water, and mix well with a spoon. Cover with a dampened cloth and let stand about 30 minutes.

To make the filling, cut the mushrooms, prawns, pork, bamboo shoots, and carrot in ¼-inch dice and place in bowl. Add the salt, sugar, sesame oil, soy sauce, cornstarch, and black pepper and mix well. Set the filling aside.

Knead the dough until it is smooth and then divide it into several portions. Working with one portion at a time and keeping the others covered, roll it into a rope about 1 inch in diameter using the palms of your hands. Cut the rope into 2-inch pieces and roll out each piece into a 3½-inch round. Working as quickly as possible so that the skins do not dry out and begin to crack, place 1 tablespoon of the filling in the center of each round and fold over to form a half-moon shape, crimping edges together securely. Place the dumplings in a steamer and steam over high heat for 25 minutes. This recipe will make 60 dumplings.

Canton Tea House
1108 Stockton Street
San Francisco

Kung Pao Chicken

2 cups vegetable oil for deep-frying
$^1/_2$ cup raw peanuts
1 cup diced chicken meat ($^1/_2$-inch dice)
2 tablespoons vegetable oil
2 teaspoons finely chopped garlic
6 whole dried red chili peppers
$^1/_2$ cup chicken broth
1 cup diced bamboo shoots
$^1/_2$ cup diced bell pepper
$^1/_2$ cup diced celery
$^1/_2$ cup diced water chestnuts

Seasoning mixture for chicken
$^1/_2$ teaspoon salt
$^1/_4$ teaspoon sugar
$^1/_2$ teaspoon soy sauce
1 tablespoon white wine
$1^1/_2$ teaspoons cornstarch

Sauce
1 tablespoon hoisin sauce
2 teaspoons vinegar
2 teaspoons soy sauce
$^1/_4$ teaspoon salt
1 teaspoon sugar
1 tablespoon Oriental sesame oil
$1^1/_2$ teaspoons cornstarch

Heat the 2 cups oil in a wok or deep pan to 325°F. Deep-fry the peanuts until golden brown, remove with a slotted utensil, and drain well; set aside. (This step may be omitted if you prefer to use roasted peanuts.) Combine the chicken and its seasoning mixture and mix well; set aside. Combine all of the sauce ingredients and mix well; set aside.

Heat a wok until very hot and add the 2 tablespoons oil. When the oil is hot, add the garlic and chili pepper and stir-fry for 30 seconds. Add the chicken and stir-fry for 2 minutes. Then add the chicken broth, cover, and cook for 2 minutes. Uncover and add the bamboo shoots, bell pepper, celery, and water chestnuts and stir-fry for 1 minute. Add the sauce mixture and cook, stirring, for 30 seconds, or until the pan juices are slightly thickened. Toss in the deep-fried peanuts and serve immediately.

Yat Sing
327 First Street
Los Altos

Lemon Chicken

2 whole chicken breasts, boned and cut into 1- by 2- by $^{1}/_{2}$-inch
   pieces
1 egg yolk
$^{1}/_{4}$ teaspoon salt
$^{1}/_{4}$ teaspoon msg
1 cup tapioca starch
1 quart vegetable oil
2 lemon slices

Lemon sauce
$^{7}/_{8}$ cup white vinegar
6 tablespoons sugar
$^{1}/_{4}$ teaspoon salt
$^{1}/_{2}$ teaspoon custard powder
Juice of $^{1}/_{2}$ lemon

Place the chicken pieces in a bowl, add the egg yolk, salt, and msg, and mix well. Toss the chicken pieces in the tapioca starch so that they are well coated.

Heat the oil in a wok or deep pan to 325°F. Deep-fry the chicken until it is golden brown, about 5 minutes. While the chicken is cooking, combine all of the ingredients for the lemon sauce in a saucepan and set aside. When the chicken is done, remove it from the pan with a slotted utensil and place on a serving platter. Immediately bring the lemon sauce to a boil, stirring to dissolve the sugar, and pour over the chicken. Garnish the platter with the lemon slices and serve.

**Fung Lum
1815 South Bascom Avenue
San Jose**

Ma-Po's Bean Curd

3 cups vegetable oil
Eight 2-inch bean-curd squares, cut in $^1/_2$-inch cubes
4 ounces ground pork or beef
1 teaspoon chopped garlic
1 tablespoon hot bean paste
2 tablespoons soy sauce
1 teaspoon salt
2 cups pork or chicken broth
2 teaspoons cornstarch, mixed with
  2 teaspoons water
1 tablespoon chopped green onion
1 teaspoon Oriental sesame oil
1 tablespoon brown peppercorn powder (crushed Szechuan
  peppercorns)

Heat the oil in a wok to 325°F. Deep-fry the bean curd cubes for about 30 seconds. Remove with a slotted utensil and set aside.

Remove all but 3 tablespoons of the oil from the wok. Reheat the oil that remains, add the pork or beef and stir-fry until browned. Add the garlic, hot bean paste, soy sauce, salt, broth, and reserved bean curd and simmer for 3 minutes. Add the cornstarch-water mixture and stir until slightly thickened. Sprinkle with the green onion and sesame oil and transfer to a serving dish. Sprinkle with brown peppercorn powder and serve.

Note: If you wish a hotter dish, add hot red pepper oil to taste. You may also omit the deep-frying of the bean-curd cubes and instead cook them briefly in boiling water.

Asia Palace
885–887 Fourth Street
San Rafael

Minced Squab

2 tablespoons peanut oil
2 squabs, skinned, boned, and finely chopped
2 cloves garlic, finely minced
2 slices ginger root, minced
8 dried Chinese black mushrooms, soaked in water to soften,
   drained, and finely chopped
8 water chestnuts, finely chopped
1/4 cup bamboo shoots, finely chopped
1/4 cup sliced Virginia ham, finely chopped
1 tablespoon dark soy sauce
1 tablespoon oyster sauce
1/2 teaspoon sugar
1/2 teaspoon salt
1 teaspoon Oriental sesame oil
1/2 cup chicken broth
2 green onions, minced
2 teaspoons cornstarch, mixed with
   2 teaspoons water
8 lettuce leaves
Hoisin sauce

Heat a wok until very hot and add the oil. When the oil is hot, add the squab, garlic, and ginger and stir-fry for 2 minutes. Add the mushrooms, water chestnuts, bamboo shoots, and Virginia ham and stir-fry for 1 minute. Add the soy sauce, oyster sauce, sugar, salt, sesame oil, and chicken broth and stir-fry for 1 minute. Add the green onions and mix in. Add the cornstarch-water mixture and stir until the pan juices are slightly thickened. Transfer to a serving platter.

To serve, spoon 2 tablespoons of the minced squab mixture on each leaf of lettuce, top with 1 teaspoon of hoisin sauce, roll up, and eat out of hand.

Imperial Palace
919 Grant Avenue
San Francisco

Mongolian Lamb

$1^{1}/_{2}$ pounds boneless leg of lamb, cut in $^{1}/_{8}$-inch-thick strips
2 medium bell peppers, cut in 1- to 1-$^{1}/_{2}$-inch pieces
2 medium yellow onions, cut in 1- to 1-$^{1}/_{2}$-inch pieces
2 tablespoons vegetable oil

Marinade
Pinch of sugar
Pinch of salt
$^{1}/_{4}$ teaspoon crushed ginger root
$^{1}/_{4}$ teaspoon crushed garlic
$^{1}/_{4}$ teaspoon oyster sauce
Few drops of Oriental sesame oil
$^{1}/_{2}$ teaspoon hoisin sauce
$^{1}/_{2}$ teaspoon brown bean sauce
1 teaspoon cornstarch
$^{1}/_{4}$ teaspoon hot pepper sauce
2 tablespoons sherry
$^{1}/_{4}$ teaspoon crushed fresh coriander
$^{1}/_{4}$ teaspoon crushed green onion
Black pepper to taste

Combine all of the ingredients for the marinade in a bowl and mix well. Add the lamb to the marinade and let stand for 20 minutes. Bring a saucepan of water to a boil, add the bell pepper and onion and boil for 1 minute. Drain well and set aside.

Heat a wok until very hot and add the oil. When the oil is hot, add the lamb and its marinade and stir-fry for 20 to 30 seconds, or until meat is lightly browned. Add the bell pepper and onion and stir-fry for 15 to 20 seconds. Do not overcook. Transfer to a serving platter and serve immediately.

China Station
700 University Avenue
Berkeley

Prawns à la Szechuan

1 pound medium shrimp, shelled and deveined
1 teaspoon salt
2 tablespoons water
3 tablespoons vegetable oil
1 small slice ginger root, minced
1 clove garlic, minced
1 tablespoon chopped dried red chili pepper
1 tablespoon sherry
1 cup chicken broth
$^1/_2$ teaspoon salt
1 tablespoon soy sauce
1 tablespoon sugar
2 tablespoons catsup
1 teaspoon Oriental sesame oil
2 tablespoons cornstarch, mixed with
   2 tablespoons water
$^1/_4$ cup chopped green onion tops

Put the shrimp in a bowl, add the 1 teaspoon salt and water, and mix gently with your hands. Rinse the shrimp well under cold running water. Pat dry and set aside. (This process will not only clean the shrimp, but also whiten them.)

Heat a wok until very hot and add the oil. When the oil is hot, add the ginger and garlic and brown for a few seconds. Add the shrimp and chili pepper, and while stir-frying, add the sherry, chicken broth, $^1/_2$ teaspoon salt, soy sauce, sugar, catsup, sesame oil, and cornstarch-water mixture. Continue stir-frying until well blended and pan juices are slightly thickened. Add green onion, toss lightly, and serve.

The Mandarin
900 North Point
San Francisco

Sautéed Clams in Garlic Sauce

2 pounds fresh clams in the shell
2 tablespoons vegetable oil
1 cup hot water
2 green onions, diced
1 tablespoon diced red chili pepper

Garlic sauce
$1/2$ teaspoon crushed garlic
$1/4$ teaspoon crushed ginger root
Pinch of sugar
Few drops Oriental sesame oil
$1^1/4$ teaspoons cornstarch
Black pepper to taste

Combine all of the ingredients for the garlic sauce and set aside. Bring a pot of water to a boil, add clams, and cook for 20 to 30 seconds, or until clams are half open. Drain clams well and set aside.

Heat a wok until very hot and add the oil. Add the garlic sauce and the hot water, mix well, and add the clams. Stir-fry for 10 to 15 seconds and mix in the green onions and red peppers. Transfer to a serving platter and serve immediately.

China Station
700 University Avenue
Berkeley

Shrimp with Lobster Sauce

2 tablespoons vegetable oil
6 ounces ground pork
1 teaspoon finely chopped ginger root
2 green onions, finely chopped
1 ounce salted black beans, rinsed in cold water, drained, and
   mashed to a paste
6 ounces raw prawns, shelled and deveined
1 teaspoon sugar
1 teaspoon soy sauce
1/2 teaspoon oyster sauce
1/2 teaspoon msg
1/2 teaspoon Oriental sesame oil
1 cup chicken broth
2 eggs, beaten

Heat a wok until very hot and add the oil. When the oil is hot, add the pork, ginger, and green onion and stir-fry for 2 minutes. Add the mashed black beans and prawns and stir-fry for 2 minutes. Then add the sugar, soy sauce, oyster sauce, msg, sesame oil, and chicken broth, bring to a boil, and cook for 1 minute. Stir in the beaten egg, mix well just until set, and serve.

Ruby Palace
631 Kearny Street
San Francisco

Sweet and Sour Crispy Pork Tenderloin

^{1}/2 pound pork tenderloin or pork chop meat, cut in bite-size pieces
1 egg white, lightly beaten
3 tablespoons soy sauce
4^1/2 tablespoons cornstarch
2 cups vegetable oil

Sweet and sour sauce
^{1}/2 pound sugar
4 tablespoons vinegar
^{1}/2 tablespoon salt
1 cup water
2^1/2 tablespoons cornstarch, mixed with
   2 tablespoons water

Combine pork, egg white, soy sauce, and cornstarch in a bowl and mix well. Combine all of the ingredients for the sweet and sour sauce, except the cornstarch-water mixture, in a small saucepan and set aside.

Heat the oil in a wok to 325°F. Deep-fry the pork pieces for 10 minutes, then remove with a slotted utensil and transfer to a warmed serving platter. Bring the sauce mixture to a boil and stir in the cornstarch-water mixture. Cook, stirring, for 30 seconds, or until thickened. Pour the sauce over the pork and serve immediately.

Asia Garden
772 Pacific Avnue
San Francisco

Sweet and Sour Pork

1 pound lean pork, cut in bite-size pieces
1 tablespoon sherry
1 tablespoon soy sauce
1 egg, lightly beaten
1 tablespoon cornstarch
3 tablespoons flour
Vegetable oil for deep-frying
3 tablespoons vegetable oil
1 small onion, quartered
3 bell peppers, quartered
1 clove garlic, minced
3 slices canned pineapple, drained and quartered

Sauce
1/3 cup sugar
4 tablespoons catsup
1 tablespoon sherry
2 tablespoons vinegar
4 tablespoons soy sauce
1 tablespoon cornstarch, mixed with
   1/3 cup water

Mix together the pork, sherry, soy sauce, egg, cornstarch, and flour. Heat the oil for deep-frying in a wok or deep pan to 325°F. Deep-fry the pork until well done and crisp on the edges. Remove with a slotted utensil to an ovenproof platter covered with paper toweling and place in a low oven to keep warm. To make the sauce, combine the sugar, catsup, sherry, vinegar, and soy sauce and mix well. Then mix in the cornstarch-water mixture until well blended; set aside.

Heat a wok until very hot and add the 3 tablespoons oil. When the oil is hot, add the onion, bell peppers, and garlic and stir-fry briefly. Add the sauce mixture, stirring constantly until slightly thickened. Add the fried pork and pineapple, mix well, and serve immediately.

Kee Joon's
433 Airport Boulevard
Burlingame

West Lake Duck

One 5-pound duck
1^1/$_2$ tablespoons soy sauce
1 quart vegetable oil
2 ounces star anise, crushed
1 teaspoon salt
1 teaspoon sugar
1 teaspoon white wine
1^1/$_4$ cups chicken broth
1 tablespoon vegetable oil
1 ounce chopped ginger root
2 green onions, finely chopped
1 pound lettuce or spinach, cut in 2-inch pieces
1 tablespoon cornstarch, mixed with
   2 tablespoons water

Wash the duck and pat dry. Rub the soy sauce in the cavity and on the outside of the duck. Heat the oil for deep-frying in a wok to 400°F. Deep-fry the duck until golden brown, turning the duck as necessary to brown on all sides. Remove the duck to a shallow plate and sprinkle with the star anise, salt, sugar, and white wine. Pour the chicken broth over the duck, place the duck in a steamer, and steam for 1^1/$_2$ hours, or until tender.

Just before the duck is cooked, heat a wok until very hot and add the 1 tablespoon oil. When the oil is hot, add the ginger, green onions, and lettuce or spinach and stir-fry for 2 minutes. Transfer the stir-fried vegetables to a serving platter and place the duck on top of them. Pour the juices that have accumulated from cooking the duck into a saucepan and bring to a boil. Add the cornstarch-water mixture and cook, stirring, for 30 seconds. Pour this sauce over the duck and serve.

Ruby Palace
631 Kearny Street
San Francisco

EARLY MORNING RESTAURANTS

San Francisco	*Location*	*Opening Time*
EASTERN BAKERY	720 Grant Avenue Chinatown	8:00 A.M.
GOLDEN DRAGON NOODLE SHOP	833 Washington Street Chinatown	7:00 A.M.
JUNMAE GUEY	1222 Stockton Street Chinatown	8:00 A.M.

Oakland		
ON ON	702 Webster Street Chinatown	8:00 A.M.

LATE EVENING RESTAURANTS

San Francisco	*Location*	*Closing Time*
GOLDEN DRAGON NOODLE SHOP	833 Washington Street Chinatown	1:00 A.M.
IMPERIAL PALACE	919 Grant Avenue Chinatown	1:00 A.M., Sunday–Thursday 2:00 A.M., Friday and Saturday
KAM LOK RESTAURANT	834 Washington Street Chinatown	midnight
OCEAN GARDEN	735 Jackson Street Chinatown	1:00 A.M.
SUN HUNG HEUNG	744 Washington Street Chinatown	midnight, Wednesday– Monday
TONG KEE #1	854 Washington Street Chinatown	1:00 A.M.
YUET LEE	1300 Stockton Street Chinatown	3:00 A.M., Wednesday– Monday

East Bay

Berkeley

CHINA STATION	700 University Avenue	2:00 P.M.

Oakland

BOK SEN	710 Webster Street Chinatown	11:30 P.M.

INDEX OF RESTAURANTS BY REGION AND CUISINE

San Francisco

East Bay

Marin County

MANDARIN

Napa County

CANTONESE AND AMERICAN

South Bay

CANTONESE

MANDARIN

CANTONESE AND MANDARIN

HAKKA

SZECHUAN

ALPHABETICAL INDEX
OF RESTAURANTS

RECIPE INDEX

ABOUT THE AUTHORS

Jennie Low is the author of the popular homestyle Chinese cook-book, *Chopsticks, Cleaver and Wok.* Born in Hong Kong, she has lived for over twenty years in the San Francisco Bay Area, currently residing in El Cerrito. Mrs. Low is well known as an instructor of Chinese cooking, having taught for fourteen years. She has, over the years, introduced many students to the pleasures of Chinese cuisine, from the popular diem sum lunch to the elegant many-course banquet, and has guided the un-initiated to the best Chinese restaurants in the Bay Area. She has also led tours to the People's Republic of China. Mrs. Low continues to teach and give cooking demonstrations as she prepares her second cookbook, which will feature her favorite Szechuan recipes.

Diane Yee is a curriculum resource teacher in Oakland and consul-tant for a major educational textbook company. Born in Hawaii, she has lived in the San Francisco Bay Area for over ten years, currently residing in Kensington. Diane has developed various curriculum units, including some on Chinese food, and is the author of *Gung Hay Fat Choy,* a Chi-nese cultural resource book for parents and teachers. Mrs. Yee teaches a course on Chinese culture and food and has taken students, parents, and teachers on study trips to the Bay Area's Chinatowns. She has also led an Educators' tour to the People's Republic of China.

Other California Guides from:

PRESIDIO ꓕ PRESS

☐ **ROBERT FINIGAN'S GUIDE TO DISCRIMINATING** $6.95
DINING IN SAN FRANCISCO

One of America's foremost restaurant and wine critics
presents San Francisco's most distinctive gastronomic
experiences.

☐ **THE GREAT CABLE CAR ADVENTURE BOOK** $6.95

Jill Losson and Gene Anthony

A tour of San Francisco via the famous cable cars—a
guide with maps and photos.

☐ **MAKING THE MOST OF MARIN** $7.95

Patricia Arrigoni; photographs by Michael Bry

Across the Golden Gate Bridge to beautiful Marin
County—an insider's guide.

And from Margot Patterson Doss—A series of walking
guides by San Francisco's well-known walker/writer/teacher:

☐ **BAY AREA AT YOUR FEET** $7.95

☐ **GOLDEN GATE PARK AT YOUR FEET** $4.95

☐ **THERE, THERE: EAST SAN FRANCISCO BAY AT YOUR** $6.95
FEET

Ask for at your favorite bookstore, or order from Presidio Press,
P.O. Box 892CR, Novato, CA 949480892; telephone: (415) 883-1373.
When ordering, please include $1.75 for shipping and handling
(California residents add appropriate sales tax).
Presidio Press honors Master Charge, Visa, and American Express.
Include card number and expiration date.